As I read Fred Franklin's book on the love Larry had for Justin, part of the words to a song sung in 1957 by Jim Reeves seemed to fit this story.

> Where does a broken heart go
> when it dies of pain?
> Is there a heaven for broken hearts?
> Will it live again?

Fred mentions several instances of driving down to the Ouachita River. Brother Troy Chapman, when he was pastor at Spencer Baptist Church, once told me, "Have you ever noticed when you're troubled, there is peace and comfort in riding down and sitting by the river." I thought of all this as Fred told the story of Billy Tom and him in driving to the Hooker Hole to sit and talk as adulthood was approaching.

Fred Franklin's caring and tender heart shows through continually as he carries us back to special years and people in our lives.

This is a book to read over again, and to give to your children and grandchildren. I'm honored to write this for my special friend since 7th grade, Fred Franklin. Thanks for the walk through the time when we were teenagers. Through Fred's book, Larry will always be "Forever Young."

Fred Franklin was one of the best natural athletes in high school I've ever known. I think he is an even better storyteller.

Bobby Jenny
Linville High School
Class of '63

I Can't Stop Loving You

Franklin

First published by Dog Ear Publishing
4011 Vincennes Road
Indianapolis, IN 46268
www.dogearpublishing.net

ISBN: 978-1-4575-6315-7

This book is printed on acid free paper.
Printed in the United States of America

Table of Contents

CHAPTER 1

Summer, 1958

LARRY WAYNE SCARBOROUGH had been working in his dad's chicken houses all morning and he was tired and dirty. But he had plans to go to Bastrop today, so he took a bath, shook some Wild Root hair oil into the palm of his left hand, rubbed his hands together, and then rubbed it into his hair. His hair was still damp from the scrubbing he gave it, and the hair oil only caused it to curl up more, and after combing through it, it remained tousled looking, but it was an orderly tousle, if there is such a thing.

He left the house and headed down the dirt drive that would lead to the graveled road toward Haile. He glanced up through the treetops that extended out over the narrow road, a reaction to the rolling thunder that seemed to come from far away as it caught up with and passed him. He hoped it wouldn't rain, but if it did, he hoped it would not begin before he came to the highway at Haile.

But the rain did begin, before he had walked another hundred yards, just as he turned right on the graveled road. It was a thunderstorm that lasted long enough to get Larry soaking wet and long enough to wet the red clay topping along the sides of the road to a depth of a half inch.

"Dang it," Larry said aloud as he began slipping on the wet clay, the slipping ending after a few steps as the clay began to stick to the bottom of his shoes, and it built up thicker with each step he took. His feet got heavier as the buildup of mud got thicker and then it began to get wider and interfere with his walking.

"Sticky crap," he mumbled as he crossed the ditch on his right and raked his shoes on a low limb of a pine sapling in the edge of the woods, leaving globs of the sticky red clay hanging from the limb. He turned and stopped before crossing back over the ditch. He looked down the road to see if he could walk alongside of it, but he realized that because of the tall grass, walking there would make his pants legs wetter still. He decided to contend with the buildup of mud and wipe the bottoms of his shoes each time it became necessary. He was almost in front of Jake Parker's house now, and the highway was less than a quarter mile away.

After crossing the railroad tracks adjacent to the highway, Larry turned right and crossed the highway, walking the short distance to Ed Thomas's store. He wanted to see if Billy George McKinnie was there yet because they had plans to hitchhike to Bastrop to the drive in and the skating rink, where they could always find some girls to flirt with.

Billy George was not there, so Larry walked the couple hundred feet to Brown's Grocery & Post Office, to see if he might be there. Sure enough, when he walked into the store, there sat Billy George, along with Sidney Ray. Ferris Brown, the postmaster for the little community, was inside the small room that was the "Post Office", in the right back corner of the store. He looked over the top of his glasses through the small service window as Larry came into the store, but didn't speak. Ferris's brother, Jim Ollie Brown, spoke to Larry as he walked in and sat down in one of the chairs in the middle of the building. The chairs were equally spaced around a tall, natural gas space heater that men would hover over when the winter chilled the building, talking politics, boxing, hunting, or whatever local gossip may be passing around at the time.

Jim Ollie was the Justice of the Peace for Ward 8 of Union Parish, and his father before him had been the Justice. He was a bachelor, and today, as usual, he had traces of snuff running down his chin from each corner of his mouth. Jim Ollie would always look over his bifocals as he talked to you. Ferris only wore his glasses when he worked the Post Office, but Jim Ollie always had his bifocals on. Ferris was also a snuff-dipper, as was the third brother, Anna, who worked up the highway at the Haile Sawmill. The Brown brothers were good men and they were well liked by everyone in the community, but some jokingly laughed about their habit of snuff dipping, and occasionally, you would hear someone say, "Ferris dips snuff, Jim Ollie wears snuff, and Anna eats it".

"Are y'all ready to hit the road toward Bastrop?" Billy George asked Larry after they had visited for a few minutes. Sidney had asked to go along with the other two, so Billy George pointed and motioned for him to come.

"Heck Yeah", said Larry, as he let out a short laugh, or giggle....it was kind of a mixture of the two that was unlike anyone else's laugh, and there was no mistaking who it was when you heard that laugh.

The three of them walked out of the store and began walking south along the highway that led from Haile through Spencer and Sterlington. The clouds from the thunderstorm were dissipating and the sun was peeping through the clouds now. Instead of standing out in front of the stores in Haile to wait for a ride, they began walking and had gone a couple hundred yards down the highway before they heard a vehicle beyond the sharp curve in the highway in front of the Brown Brothers store. They stopped and each of them stuck their right hands out in front of them, thumbs up, as a car approached and slowed to a stop in front of them.

There were two young men in the car, and the one on the passenger side rolled the window down and told the boys to get in, as he pointed to the back seat. He opened his door and stepped out of the car and flipped his seat back forward so they could get in. "It's gonna be kinda tight for y'all, and one of you needs to hold that box of cheese in your lap", he said as he pointed to a round, wooden crate with a wooden cover on the top lying on the back seat.

Larry got in first, picking up the box, then he gave it to Sidney as he got in and scooted in beside him, followed by Billy George. The young man, who the boys recognized as a man with last name of Fowler, flipped the seat back after the boys were seated, got back in and shut the door. Fowler reached into his front pocket and pulled out a pocketknife as the car started moving, and he handed the knife over the seatback to Billy George. "Here, y'all cut you some of that hoop cheese in that box, if you like cheese".

All of them agreed that they liked cheese, and Sidney removed the cover from the box, revealing about a fourth of what once was a ten pound, round block of cheese about six inches tall. Billy George opened the knife and sliced off a chunk of the cheese and handed it over to Larry, and then did the same for Sidney before cutting off some for himself. "Where did y'all get this good cheese", Billy George asked as he flipped the knife blade shut and handed the knife back up front to Fowler.

The driver, a man named Bowen, laughed as he replied, "We bought all the cheese that this storekeeper in Marion had left. We already had a half case of cold beer and man, you got to have some good cheese to go with your beer! Y'all want a beer?"

"Boy, that would be good", Larry said, and there went that funny little laugh of his again, but the others declined the offer.

Fowler reached into the cardboard beer box and pulled out a beer, handing it over the seatback to Larry. "Now don't tell nobody that we gave you a beer! You can tell them we gave you cheese, but we don't want nobody scolding our butts about the beer!"

The car got quiet as the boys ate cheese and Larry drank his beer, and the sound of the radio drowned out the roar of the tires on the bumpy blacktop, as Bowen reached over and turned up the volume as Conway Twitty's song *It's Only Make Believe* came on. No-one said another word until the song ended.

Fowler spoke up as soon as the song was over. "Boy, I love that song! That Conway Twitty is my favorite singer. You know, I read somewhere that he wanted to be a professional baseball player, but he got hurt, or something, and so he started singing. I'll bet he's glad he did now! He's making a ton of money, just with that one song!"

They all agreed with Fowler, and little else was said until they crossed the river bridge at Sterlington and Bowen asked the boys where they were headed. When they told him they were going to Bastrop, he replied, "I figured y'all were just coming here to Sterlington. We are going to Monroe, so we can either let y'all out here, or we can drop you off down the highway, at the intersection."

"Just drop us off here at Strawberry's café. Somebody will stop in here on their way to Bastrop," Larry said. "We sure appreciate the ride."

"Yeah, and we really appreciate the cheese!" said Billy George, and Sidney also thanked them for the ride and the cheese.

"You're welcome", replied Bowen. "Y'all be careful, and don't do anything I wouldn't do," he said with a laugh as he pulled the car over in front of the café and Fowler opened the door and let the boys out. As the car pulled back onto the highway, the boys walked to the door and went inside the café.

Billy George, tall and slim, with a touch of red in his hair, led the way as they entered the café and went over to sit on the stools that lined the counter. They ordered cokes and Larry went over to the juke box and dropped a coin in it and after searching through the listing of songs, he punched the number for Jerry Lee Lewis' song *Whole Lot of Shaking Going On*. Larry liked this song, and he thought about Billy Tom Ellis, who would sing this song sometimes down by the smoking bench at school. Billy Tom knew the song by heart and during recess periods at Linville High, many times he would sing it while sitting on the circular wooden "smoking bench" under some oak trees near the baseball field. He would do a fantastic acapella version of it for the other boys who were present. Doc Cooper, the agriculture and shop teacher, as part of shop class, had his students make the bench and place it there, and the older boys were allowed to smoke at this location on their breaks from classes.

There was no-one in the café the boys knew, but they were sure of one thing, that being, on a Saturday afternoon, there would soon be someone come in they did know. More than likely, that someone would be headed to Bastrop, and sure enough, they didn't have to wait long.

It was Grady Williamson who walked through the door, a man a good bit older than the boys, and they knew him well. Grady was a friendly guy who was easy to talk to. He had a laid back personality, and he spoke to them, calling each of them by name. "What are y'all up to?" he asked.

"We're headed for skating rink in Bastrop....looking for a ride", said Larry.

"Well by golly, I'm headed to Bastrop myself", he said. "Y'all are welcome to ride with me. I'm just going to get me a cup of coffee, so I won't be here very long".

They were pleased to hear this, and happy that their wait for a ride was a short one. Larry went back to the jukebox and dropped another coin in, punched the number to play *Rebel Rouser* by Duane Eddy, and they listened while Grady sipped his coffee.

After Grady finished his coffee, he paid at the counter, turned to the boys and said, "Load up, fellers". They followed Grady out to the car, Larry getting in the front, while Billy George and Sidney climbed into the back seat. As he pulled the car out on the road, Grady said, "I saw that ole tall white headed roughneck from Calhoun in Haile just now. I don't know his name….he's got some nickname they call him, don't he?"

"Yeah, I don't know his name, but I think they call him Cotton," said Billy George from the back seat.

"Uh huh," said Sidney. "I heard another one of that crew he works with last week say that Cotton was as crazy as a run-over dog! I don't know what that means, but I guess he must be pretty crazy!" They all had a good laugh at the comment.

Grady was still laughing a minute later when he asked the boys where they were going in Bastrop.

"We want to go to Joe's Drive-In first, and after that, we're going on into town to the skating rink," said Larry. "Unless we get hooked up at Joe's."

"O.K, I'll drop y'all off and then I'll go right back down the highway to that bar, and if you decide to go to the skating rink, walk down there and get me and I'll take y'all into town. If I don't see y'all in, say, about an hour, I'm probably going to head back to Union Parish."

"That sounds like a good deal," said Billy George.

It was almost sundown when they arrived at Joe's, and after Grady let them out there and drove back toward the bar, the three of them walked up to the drive-in window and ordered cokes, then sat down nearby at one of the small tables, sipping their drinks. They saw a few familiar faces, but no-one that they really knew very well, so they just made small talk for a while, hoping to see some girls they knew.

Darkness began to settle in, and all the lights around the drive-in seemed to get brighter. Larry saw that the other two were beginning to get a little bit restless, so he stood up, stretched, and looked back down the highway toward the beer joint. "Everybody must be at the skating rink," he said. "Let's go down there and root Grady out of that joint. He said he'd take us to the rink."

Sidney stood up next and punched Billy George lightly on the shoulder. "Come on, let's go get Grady." So they headed out to the shoulder of the road and walked the few minutes it took them to get to the bar.

Billy George looked to be the oldest in the group, so the others elected him to go in and get Grady. He went through the door and was gone for several minutes, while the others stood out front waiting.

Grady came out first, wiping the back of his hand across his mouth. "I apologize for holding y'all up," he told the two boys waiting just outside the door. "I had to finish my beer first. They charge too much for the darn things anyway!"

They loaded into the car, and Grady waited for the busy Saturday night traffic to clear before pulling onto the highway that would take them further into Bastrop. Grady observed the 35 MPH speed limit as he drove, chatting with the boys before turning right at the traffic light by the high school, then he was silent as he drove the few blocks to the highway that would take them to the skating rink. He dimmed his headlights shortly after turning left on the highway because he saw the glow of headlights from around a sharp curve a couple hundred yards ahead.

Sidney had closed his eyes as soon as he had gotten into the back seat of the car, directly behind the driver, and he had been half asleep since they pulled out of the drive in parking lot. Billy George was on the other side in back, with Larry up front with Grady. There was silence as Grady picked up speed, shooting for fifty miles per hour, the speed limit on this loop around the downtown area of town.

As the vehicle they had seen the glow of headlights coming from beyond the curve suddenly appeared in the curve going at a high rate of speed, Grady stated quickly, "Boy, he needs to slow that thing down!" And as soon as he said it, the oncoming vehicle's right front tire dropped off the edge of the pavement, onto the graveled shoulder, and when the driver over corrected as he jerked the wheels back onto the blacktop, the rear end slid outwards on the shoulder. The vehicle was sliding sideways toward them and they could see that it was a pickup truck, so Grady grunted loudly as he slammed on his brakes. It was too late to slow down much at all before the truck fishtailed and slammed almost head-on into Grady's car.

The loud crash and the sound of breaking glass woke Sidney up from his near-sleep as he was thrown into the seat in front of him, his head hitting Grady in his back.....hard. Grady had both hands on the steering wheel, gripping so tightly that Sidney's collision with him didn't move him forward enough to cause serious injury, but his face did hit the steering wheel hard enough to cause some bruises.

Billy George had thrown both his arms up in front of him in order to try to stop his forward motion toward the seat in front of him, and he received a cut on one of his hands, a cut that he did not know how it occurred.

Larry was thrown face-first into the windshield in front of him, and the glass shattered, but the car's windshield had a layer of clear plastic sandwiched between two layers of glass, and Larry's face was cut up severely as it only stretched the plastic outward as both layers of glass shattered. The shattered glass on the inside of the windshield was trapped by the plastic, causing the many pieces of glass to be ground into Larry's face. This layer of plastic was designed as a safety feature to keep people from being thrown out of the car through the windshield in the event of a collision. But in early results such as this one, it was found that the design sometimes caused more severe cuts than windshields without the plastic layer. In newer cars, the design of the plastic layer would be made thinner and results improved as time passed.

As all the occupants of both vehicles piled out onto the highway, one of the pickup's headlights was still shining, giving enough light for them to see each other, and everybody, including the pickup truck's driver and his passenger were shocked at the amount of blood pouring from Larry's face. The driver of the truck quickly un-buttoned his shirt and pulled it off, then folded it up to a size approximately the size of Larry's face. He rushed up to Larry and pressed the shirt up to his face, instructing Larry to hold it to his face in order to slow the bleeding.

Grady went over to the open door of his car where Larry had been riding, and as he began to brush the shattered glass off the seat with his hand, he noted that the seat had some blood on it. He opened the glove box and pulled out a clean mechanic's wiping cloth to clean the seat before he called for Larry to come sit down there. Billy George led Larry over and backed him up to the seat and helped him sit on the side of it, with his feet resting on the pavement by the car.

The driver of the pickup was apologizing again and again, and he kept saying his front tire had dropped off the edge of the blacktop pavement into the loose gravel, causing him to lose control of his truck. "I shouldn't have been driving so fast!" he kept saying. "Man, I'm so sorry," he said to Larry. "I'm sorry!"

He then turned to Grady and the others. "I'm sorry! Are y'all alright? Any of you hurt? Lord, I hope not!"

"My face is a little bunged up, but I don't think it drew any blood," said Grady. "What about y'all? He asked as he turned toward the other boys.

Billy George held out his left hand, showing Grady the blood. "I got a cut on my hand, but it's not too bad. I'll be alright, but we need to get Larry to the hospital to get some stiches!"

Michael Varnell, the young man who was the passenger riding in the truck that crashed into them, introduced himself and told Billy George that a man stopped immediately after the collision, telling him that he would go to the small store just beyond the scene of the accident and call the police and tell them to get an ambulance out here.

"O.K., that's good. The ambulance will probably be here shortly then! Boy, they need to come on, because Larry is really bleeding bad!" Billy George replied.

Sidney had said he guessed he was alright, as he leaned his rear end against the side of Grady's car. "What in the world happened?" he asked nobody in particular. He had been so near asleep when the impact of the crash woke him up, he was still in a minor state of shock, as he put his hand up to his forehead, feeling the bruise above his eyes.

The driver of the pickup introduced himself as Petey Carroll, and told them he lived in Bastrop. He began to apologize again for the accident, but was interrupted by the distant sound of a siren. "Man, it's about time that ambulance got here!" he said, as he returned to Larry's side.

"The hospital here in Bastrop is a good one, and they will take good care of you," Petey told Larry. "They will probably want to keep you there at least overnight, but if they keep you a day or so, I will be checking on you and I can get anything you need as long as you are there.

"The siren that Petey Carroll had heard turned out to be Bastrop police car that arrived on the scene before the ambulance got there and the police officer quickly ascertained that there was no pressing emergency to the injured from the accident, even though he was concerned about Larry. He saw that the bleeding from Larry's injuries was being controlled to a certain extent, so he began to question all involved in the accident in order to find what charges needed to be filed. Petey Carroll immediately told the policeman that the accident was completely his fault. The policeman asked for Petey's driver's license so he could begin his report.

Larry thanked Petey for the use of his shirt as the policeman was getting his report booklet to begin writing up his report.

"I appreciate it," said Larry as he pressed the bloody shirt from one cut to the other in order to wipe up the blood oozing from the many cuts on his face. He then laughed as he looked down at the shirt and told Petey, "I don't think you'll wear this shirt again!"

"No, probably not, but I don't care," Petey replied, laughing along with Larry. "I'm glad I was wearing that soft cotton shirt, instead of an old work shirt." He turned and looked back toward town as the ambulance appeared coming around the curve where he had lost control of his vehicle. "There comes your ride," he said.

During the three days following the accident, Petey Carroll probably spent more time with Larry at the Bastrop Hospital than Larry's parents did, as he visited at least two times each day, bringing him a toothbrush, toothpaste, and snacks to supplement the not so great hospital food. Petey was so remorseful for causing Larry's injuries, and also the minor injuries to Larry's friends, and in the ensuing months, they would all become good friends.

It took several weeks before Larry's facial cuts were healed enough that he did not have to apply healing ointment to his face, but many of the scars were raised marks that would be with him for life, and they would actually give his handsome face character, in a way, instead of being a terrible disfigurement.

Life for Larry soon became the same old routine for him, with work on the farm, doing much of the work involved in the raising of the chickens. Larry seemed to be more popular after the wreck, for reasons that seemed to escape him, but he enjoyed the extra attention.

CHAPTER 2

Summer & Fall of 1959

I HAD THE pleasure during the summer of loading and hauling hay for some of the local cattle farmers who hired Elmer Wilson and his son, Walter, to cut and bale their hay. This was my only chance of earning some money during the summer, and in addition to the work, I got to hear some interesting stories from the older guys working with us.

My friend, Billy Tom Ellis's grandfather and my grandfather were brothers, and his mother and my mother first cousins, so he and I were what? Second cousins? I don't know, but we were both afflicted with rambling fever. My brother Gerald and Billy Tom were the same age, with me being one year younger, but it was Billy Tom and me who ran together and stayed on the move.

Billy Tom had worked during the summer for Gordon Turner at the Alabama Landing on the Ouachita River about two miles beyond our farm. Fishing was really good on the river and Billy Tom helped the fishermen launch their boats into the river, plus helping them load their gear into the boats, and then helping them load out when they came back in later in the day. At the top of the high bank up from the landing, there was a small shack that served as a store where you could buy cold drinks, candy, chips, a few canned grocery items, and cigarettes or snuff. Billy Tom helped work the store when there were no boats to be launched.

He was saving his money in hopes of buying a decent used car as soon as he was old enough to drive.

It was early September, not long after school had begun, my first contact with Larry Scarborough came about one day as I was walking by the eighth grade classroom on my way to the gymnasium. Larry came up from behind me on the sidewalk, and as he got beside me on my left, he grabbed my left bicep and clamped down with his thumb on the outside of my arm and with the ends of his fingers on the underside. There was instant pain that scared me, for I had no idea what was causing this sharp pain. Larry forced me to walk along beside him for a few yards along the sidewalk, because his grip on my arm convinced me that there would be no escaping from him. After that few yards, Larry laughed at my moaning, and as I asked just what in the world was it that he had that was causing my pain, he released his grip on my arm.

There was instant relief, and as Larry continued to laugh at me, he held his right hand up for me to see........he had taken fingernail clippers or a pocketknife and cut his fingernails into saw like teeth, with very sharp points on them......wicked looking weapons.

"I'm sorry," said Larry. "I didn't mean to hurt you......I guess I gripped a little too tightly!"

"Yeah, I guess so," I said. "I didn't know what had a hold on me!" I laughed then and told Larry that everything was alright.

"Good," he said, and again told me he was sorry.

It's funny sometimes how a friendship begins, but this was the first time I think that Larry had even noticed that I was alive, and I don't remember ever having any contact with him before that day. It wasn't long after that experience that I began to develop a friendship with him that would, in time, grow into a close friendship.

It was early October when a group of us boys who gathered in Haile on Saturday night were talking about doing something to liven up our time together, and since several of our families had horses, we made plans for the following Saturday to ride our horses into Haile. We really didn't have a plan, but it sounded like fun to us, so there was about a half-dozen of us who agreed to join in on this adventure.

Billy Tom's father had Dollie, the red mule that he used to plow their large garden with, and Billy Tom and his brothers rode Dollie a lot around Dean Community, so he made plans to ride her into Haile the following weekend. We had a paint plow horse that was not a big horse, and we rode him, but he was so lazy that the only thing we could do was walk the horse when we rode him. Billy Tom and I decided to team up and ride to Haile together the next Saturday afternoon.

We made the trip to Haile, and it was a slow journey because of my lazy horse, but we finally made it to Haile, and there we found the others waiting on us. There was Billy George McKinnie and Larry Scarborough, plus two or three others who joined in to ride.

We rode around Haile with little or no real plan as to what we were going to do, and as darkness began to fall, we gathered up across the railroad tracks where there were some open lots, and we dismounted to take a break and plan our next move.

While we were standing around in a circle discussing our options, Larry suggested that we ride south of Haile alongside of the highway, then hide in the woods at some point, while one of us went out to the highway and pretended to be hitch-hiking. When someone stopped to pick up the hitch-hiker, the rest of the group would break out of the woods and surround the car. In doing such a stunt today, you may expect to scare the person stopping, but in those days, it was pretty safe, because it was really peaceful and safe in most areas of the rural South.

When we mounted up and rode down to the highway, turning left along the pavement, the group wanted to run the horses between the railroad track and the highway. I began kicking my horse with the heels of my boots as soon as we turned south and I actually got the horse into a slow gallop. The others yelled in surprise and congratulations to me, and as my cowboy hat flew off my head, someone yelled for me to keep going, telling me that they would retrieve my hat. They didn't want me to stop because I had been using a switch and kicking my horse's ribs while we were riding together before this, and the horse had only gotten into a faster walk once during that time. They were excited to see my horse galloping, and so was I, because he had never before gone faster than the fast walk that had happened earlier on that day.

We were surprised to find a huge mound of dirt about a quarter mile south of Jordan's Grocery, near the edge of the woods and just across the shallow ditch along the highway. The mound was covered in brush that blended in with the scrub trees on each side and behind the dirt mound, and the trees were not growing so close together to keep us from riding our horses in between them. This was the perfect place to hide us from view of anyone driving by on the highway, so we decided to send someone out to the road to pretend to be hitch-hiking while the rest of us, still mounted on our horses except for Billy Tom on his red mule, and our decoy's horse tied to a white oak sapling near the back of the mound. Someone in the group suggested that the hitch-hiker should try to get a driver who was headed north to stop because we were pretty well completely hidden from view when coming from the south, but someone could possibly see us if they were coming from the other direction.

I don't recall who our decoy was, but after we decided that we were all hidden well enough behind the mound, he went out beside the highway and waited for a vehicle driving north to come along.

We waited less than fifteen minutes before we heard a vehicle coming up the highway, and with great anticipation, we were hoping our plan worked out well. When we heard the car stop, Larry whispered loudly, "Let's go!"

And we went tearing out of the woods, with a couple riding up and over the mound of dirt, while the others went around each side, and we were yelling like a bunch of outlaws as we surrounded the vehicle.

The car in the highway was the most beautiful 1959 Chevrolet convertible I had ever seen, white in color, with the top down, and with the little moonlight on that night, plus the headlights from the car bouncing some light off the horses in front of the car, we could see well enough to know that the driver was a stranger to us. The driver of the car was really shocked and surprised, and not knowing what to make of this, he held both arms up and yelled, "Whoa! I give up!"

We all laughed and Larry told him hastily, "This is not a robbery! We are just having some fun. We didn't mean to scare you."

"Thank God," the driver said. "I thought I had ridden into a bunch of outlaws, just like in the old west!"

We laughed again at his reaction, and someone asked the driver his name. The driver appeared to be in his late twenties, a nice looking young man, and when he told us his name, none of us had ever heard of him. But we talked with him about ten minutes, mostly telling him what a pretty car he was driving, and asking all sorts of questions about the car and the engine and how fast it would go.

We found out the young man was from Monroe, and he was driving up to see some relatives near the town of Marion. He told us that he enjoyed our short visit, and he said that most of all, he was glad we didn't rob him, and he laughed. Before he drove away, he told us to have fun and to be careful.

The night had brought with it a bit of a chill, so we decided to ride back through Haile and head on to our respective homes, as some of us had pretty long rides ahead of us. We stopped near the railroad tracks where we had gathered up before, and we talked a little while about how much fun we had this day, and about how beautiful the convertible was. Then we said our goodbyes and split up and rode away, with Billy Tom and me taking the road toward the Four Mile Post.

We had not traveled very far when Billy Tom told me that I needed to get a bigger switch and make my horse go faster than the slow walk, because, he said, we would be all night getting home.

I agreed and I stopped and dismounted, dropped my reins, and walked out into the edge of the woods and searched for a limb that was larger than the one I had been using, but not so large that I could not break it off the tree. After finding a limb that was satisfactory and breaking it off to the correct length, I walked back to my horse, climbed back up into the saddle, and I began to whip my horse on the side of his rump, but to no avail. He simply would do nothing but just plod along at a pace that seemed to be as slow as a turtle.

After we had ridden about a half mile at this slow pace, Billy Tom threatened to leave me behind and go on home without me because he could be home in less than thirty minutes. Dollie still had a lot of energy, and he said she could gallop all night long if needed. He told me once again that it would take me all night to get to my house, since my horse was so slow.

I begged Billy Tom to stay with me because I was not sure that my horse would keep going if it were not for Dollie leading the way. Billy Tom relented, but he was not happy about it, and as I look back on that night, I probably was responsible for stretching his patience as thin as it ever was in his lifetime. I apologize to you, my friend, for that long night.

When we finally reached the Four Mile Post, and Billy Tom told me good night, he loosened his bridle reins on Dollie and lightly kicked her with his heels, and immediately, she broke out into a fast gallop, and I heard the sound of her hoofs beating on the road as Billy Tom rode out of hearing in only a few minutes, because I could hear those sounds as my horse slowly plodded along, with his hoofs making a quiet, crunching sound on the roadway for the next half hour or so until we reached home at last.

It was only a week or so after this that Billy Tom and I hitchhiked to Monroe to see a movie that was filmed off the coast of California, the title was 'Operation Petticoat', and the star of the movie was Tony Curtis. A U. S. Navy ship was featured in the movie and one of the sailors on the ship was Ray Lowery, who had graduated from Linville High and he was serving in the Navy when the filming of this movie was done. Ray was seen at least one time in a scene where a group of the sailors on this ship were seen walking across the deck.

After enjoying Operation Petticoat, and walking back to the edge of town, Billy Tom and I soon caught a ride that took us all the way to Sterlington, and we began to walk toward the bridge crossing the Ouachita River between Ouachita Parish and Union Parish, along the highway that would lead to Haile. As we neared the narrow, two lane bridge spanning the river, Billy Tom said, "You know, if two big log trucks met on the bridge while we were walking across, we might get smashed against the side of the bridge and killed. I think we ought to go over the top," pointing at the steel structure above the bridge that supported the bridge's center section when it was opened to let tugboats pass through.

"You're right", I said. "Let's do it!"

So that is exactly what we did. We climbed up the steel structure over the bridge and back down the other side, a stunt that was a foolish and dangerous one for sure. Our coach at Linville High School happened to be driving into Sterlington at that time and saw us on the very top of the steel structure high above the bridge roadway below.

The following Monday at school, Coach Billy Till approached me and with an expression of wonderment on his face, asked, "What in the world were y'all doing on that bridge Saturday?"

I explained to him our reasoning for going over the top of the bridge, to eliminate the danger of being killed by big trucks meeting while we were walking across. Of course, I was laughing as I told him this.

Mr. Till said, "I was driving toward Sterlington when I saw y'all up on top of the bridge and I said to myself, who are those fools on that bridge?" Then when I got closer and I could see that it was you two, I said out loud, why, that's MY fools!"

I laughed really loudly at this and I told him, "We just thought we were taking the safest route across the bridge!"

Mr. Till only shook his head slowly and with a serious tone of voice he pleaded, "y'all please don't do anything like that again! You could have gotten killed!"

"O.K.," I said. "I think you are probably right."

CHAPTER 3

The Arrival - Spring of 1960

IN JANUARY OF 1943, five co-workers who worked for Standard Oil Company in Baton Rouge, Louisiana, were riding together in a car that ran into the rear of a stalled eighteen wheeler in the highway east of Baton Rouge. There was a heavy fog and the driver did not see the truck in time to avoid the collision, and upon impact, the car burst into flames. Three of the men managed to get out of the car and were taken to a hospital where they died a few days later from their injuries and from burns received in the crash. The other two men died in the crash. One of the men who died in the blazing car was Justin Claude Cooper, who had played football for Louisiana State University as a receiver, and he had dropped out of the university a couple of years earlier after marrying his high school sweetheart. LSU did not allow married men to play football for them at that time, so Justin only played his freshman year there. The freshmen football players were called "Baby Bengals", since LSU's mascot is the tiger. Justin was a popular and well known young man in the Baton Rouge area, a gifted athlete with a personality that made him many friends. At the time of his death, he and his wife, Marie, had a daughter named Grace Marie, who was not quite a year old, and they were expecting another child.

Four months after Justin died, on April 30, 1943, his twenty year old widow gave birth to another girl, and the grieving mother named her Justin

Claude Cooper, in honor of her deceased husband. This young wife's life was in turmoil, because eighty five days prior to her husband's death, her mother had died from injuries she suffered on the farm. She was found dead in a horse stall, with injuries to her head, and the family assumed she had been kicked by the horse.

Marie, with help from her mother in law, John Etta Kelley Cooper, shared the responsibilities of rearing Grace Marie and Justin, and five years passed before Marie would re-marry. She met and married Murphy Langrasse, a handsome construction supervisor from the Baton Rouge area, and for reasons unknown to Justin, her stepfather later changed the spelling of his last name to "Langras". A year after their marriage, Murphy and Marie presented Grace Marie and Justin with a baby sister, who they named Carolyn, and later a brother named Danny.

The Cooper girls and their step-sister and step-brother enjoyed an idyllic childhood on the Cooper farm outside of Baton Rouge, enjoying all the pleasures of life on a farm, and this included horseback riding. After a time, Marie, along with Carolyn and Danny, began traveling with Murphy when he went on the road doing construction projects around the country, while Grace Marie and Justin stayed on the farm with their Grandmother.

Trouble would come later for Marie and Murphy because of his womanizing, and Marie, with the evidence provided by a private investigator, obtained a divorce. Twelve years after the divorce, Murphy tired of the way he was living, and realizing what a sweet wife Marie had been, began seeing her again. Eventually, he convinced Marie that he could be true to her, so they remarried. Grace Marie and Justin continued living with their grandmother, John Etta. John Etta was like another mother to the girls, as they had been living with her most of their lives at that point. The Cooper girls missed their siblings as they traveled with their parents, but John Etta was good to and good for Grace Marie and Justin.

After Grace Marie and Justin were in high school in Baton Rouge, they definitely wanted to continue living with their grandmother, simply because they wanted to stay in Baton Rouge High School, a place they were familiar with, and also they both had a lot of friends there. Grace Marie presented little problems for her grandmother, but Justin was a different story. She was a free-spirited young lady, and John Etta had trouble keeping her in line. By the time Grace Marie was a senior in high school, and Justin a junior, Justin's tendency to run wild proved to be too much for her grandmother, so she contacted her brother-in-law, Sidney Cooper, who had been hired by the Union Parish School Board, in northeast Louisiana, to be the Agriculture Teacher in the small school at Linville. She asked Sidney if he and his wife would take Justin in and place her in the small school at Linville, and they agreed to help John Etta out with her problem grandchild. It was in the early spring of 1960 when Justin was brought to live in Linville, Louisiana, with her Uncle Sidney and Aunt Pearl Cooper.

No-one seems to remember exactly when, but sometime in the spring of 1960, the arrival of Justin Cooper was an event that would change the course of history for Linville High School, and in time, it would change Larry Scarborough's life completely during Justin's stay in the little community, and he would never be the same again.

After Justin arrived at Linville High, she quickly made a huge impression on most of the high school boys, and Larry was no exception. She had dark red hair, wavy and flowing down to her shoulders, and she was vivacious, with a smile that made her so popular, not only with the boys, but most of the girls wanted to be her friend. Justin's bubbly personality made her easy to like, and she would soon show everyone her wild side openly, unlike most of the local girls, whose actions in school and in public, in general, were controlled by the constraints of constant scrutiny by their parents, and most adults they came into contact with.

Students from several rural communities in the Linville area attended Linville High School, but it was not just a high school, as it was comprised of grades one through twelve, and with a grand total of barely a hundred students, there was no hiding of anything you did at school. Much of what the students did beyond the confines of school was also common knowledge to most people in the local communities. Justin Cooper's actions defied convention in many ways because girls weren't supposed to be wild in the countryside of North Louisiana, especially in the early 1960's. But Justin had been raised in the Baton Rouge area by her mother, and later by her grandmother, and they had not been able to control this free spirited girl who seemed older than her years.

When the school year ended in May of 1960, Justin returned to her Grandmother's in Baton Rouge for the summer. She returned to Linville at the end of August, 1960, to begin her senior year in high school, and it was soon after this that she began dating Larry Scarborough. Larry's father had purchased a 1956 Oldsmobile for him, and Justin jumped at the chance to date such a handsome young man who also happened to have his own car. During the previous spring while living in Linville, she had to depend on some of her girlfriends for transportation on the weekends, and Bobbie Lee Roberson was a very close friend who was much like Justin, being a free spirit with a good sense of humor. The two girls would often drive down to West Sterlington to the 'Sandpiles', an area back in the woods near the Ouachita River which was owned by a sand and gravel company. The company, in addition to their sand and gravel business, also owned a ready mix concrete company, and they had excavated huge pits for their gravel screening operation and there was so much sand generated from the gravel screening, it was left in piles that were thirty to forty feet in height. Local teenagers loved to gather there on weekend nights, and when there was a full moon they would climb up the piles and jump out as far as they could from the highest points to land maybe fifteen or twenty feet below in the soft sand, and then maybe roll or run as best they could down the steep slopes.

On most occasions, there would be some of the boys there who would have a few beers iced down in an ice chest in the trunk of their car, and they would share with others. Few of the girls would ever drink any beer, but Justin and Bobbie Lee would usually welcome an offer of a free beer or two from whoever might be sharing. Many times, someone would gather up dead limbs from along the edge of the woods across the sand road at the base of the sand piles, and they would build a fire where they could sit in the sand around the fire and drink their beer, smoke their cigarettes, and laugh and just enjoy being teenagers.

On one of those nights when Justin and Bobbie Lee were at the sand piles, Justin and Larry got together, and they trudged up one of the higher sand piles in the moonlight and sat down at the top of the pile overlooking the fire below. It took quite a bit of exertion to climb up the steep slopes, so resting at the top was a real relief in order to catch your breath before going back down. The two of them had talked some during school prior to that night, and they were just naturally attracted to each other, for obvious reasons. Justin, the beautiful redhead, with the personality that made her even more attractive, was almost immediately Larry's dream girl, unlike anyone he had ever met, with her fun loving ways.

Larry's youthful, muscular physique, the wavy hair and the handsome face, somehow made even more attractive because of the many scars from the wreck he had been in a couple of years earlier, was Justin's first choice for a boyfriend. She had dated only one other since she came to Linville, but that was for only one or two dates, going for hamburgers and cokes at Ham's Café in Sterlington.

On this night, at the top of the sand pile in the bright light of a full moon, after having had a couple of beers earlier, they sat there in the sand, talking for quite a while about each other's experiences, just getting to know one another. Finding that each of them were rebels, to a certain extent, found them reaching common ground they could relate to. Before they decided to head back down to the fire, they reached out to join hands, with Larry pulling Justin to him and they kissed as they rose to their feet. After that first kiss, their bond was almost instant, and as they stood up at the crest of the pile of sand, their silhouettes against the sky in the moonlight was seen as one by those around the fire down below, as the two soon to be lovers embraced and enjoyed another long, slow kiss. And after this, Larry grabbed Justin's left hand with his right, and with that funny little giggle/laugh, he said to her, "Let's jump as far as we can!"

They landed about twenty feet below, and they continued holding each other's hand as they ran the remaining distance to the bottom of the sand pile, falling a couple of times on the way down, rolling over in the soft sand before Larry pulled Justin back up on her feet to run again. This night was the beginning of something really special for the two of them, feelings felt by so many millions of young couples over time, as they realized they felt real love for the first time.

It was on this night at the sand piles that a romance began between Larry Scarborough and Justin Cooper that would be a classic in anyone's book when they heard the complete story of the two young lovers and the paths they would travel as they came together and were later separated by things they could not control. But the future held a hope that they would be together again, and this is where the story really begins.

Days at Linville High passed quickly the next few months for Larry and Justin, as they talked during recess periods while at school, but they had to take what they could get, because Justin's Uncle and Aunt would not allow her to go out at night during the week, unless there were school basketball games or other school functions. The weekend was their only chance to be together as they liked, and Larry would pick Justin up and they would spend most of their time driving around the area between Marion, Linville and Sterlington. Marion was about six miles north of Linville and Sterlington was about fifteen miles south. Or they might drive the graveled roads to the Ouachita River at the Alabama Landing or to another landing down river called the Hooker Hole.

On some nights they would drive to the Arkansas state line north of Marion, to a place called the State Line Café, which was, in reality, only a beer joint. The joint was an unpainted concrete block building in a clearing on the east side of the highway about one quarter mile after you entered Arkansas. The clearing was surrounded by thick woods, with no other buildings or homes nearby, and no telephone, so husbands that stayed there too late did not have to worry about their wives calling there looking for them. This was a long, long time before cell phones, but on some nights an irate wife would walk through the front door before the midnight closing time, and embarrass her husband by grabbing him by the arm and leading him out the door, and some would go meekly, but others would go under protest; but regardless, invariably, they would leave.

When Larry and Justin arrived at the beer joint, there would always be someone there that Larry knew who would purchase beer for him, and he would give them money to buy a six pack of cans of Country Club malt liquor. Larry would offer them a can for buying the malt liquor for him, and sometimes they would accept the offer, sometimes not.

Larry and Justin would head back down the highway into Louisiana and pass through Marion on their way back to Haile. They would ride the backroads as they drank their liquor, each asking so many questions about the other's past and just getting to know one another better. If they drove down to the river, they would park close enough to watch the shimmering of the water if there was any light from the moon at all. They would cuddle in the front seat of Larry's car while listening to the radio, and each of them had their favorite songs. There was little else to do in the area because it was so rural, and there were no businesses open at night within ten miles or more. It was a simple time and place in their lives that made their time together so peaceful and so enjoyable, and they grew closer quickly.

During basketball season, Larry and Justin always attended Linville's home basketball games played at night during the week, since the Coopers lived across the highway from the school, and Justin would walk over on those nights and meet Larry there after he drove the few miles from his home near Haile. Justin would keep Larry entertained at these games because she was so funny and wild and crazy, and if you were anywhere close to them in the bleachers, you would often hear that funny little laugh that was unique to Larry. The two of them enjoyed their time together at the ball games, but they wanted more. They wanted to be able to hold one another and embrace just for the warm feeling of love it generated. It is always hard for teenage lovers to keep their hands to themselves when they are together, but they had little choice at the school events. But according to Justin later, they made up for this when they were out together on weekends. Larry's love for Justin grew more and more as their relationship blossomed, and she was on his mind all of his waking hours, and Justin felt the same about Larry.

Justin developed friendships with a number of girls at Linville, but one of her closest friends was Bobbie Lee Roberson. Bobbie Lee's father allowed her to use the family car on the weekends, and she would often pick Justin up at her Uncle's house on Friday night because on Saturday nights, Justin was usually with Larry. The two girls would ride around Haile and Linville backroads, and occasionally they would drive to Marion. In Marion, they would mingle with other teenagers in the center of town around Medlin's Hardware or across the street in front of Phillip's Pharmacy. Bobbie Lee knew many of the teenagers who went to Marion High, and Justin soon developed friendships with Bobbie Lee's friends, who loved to hear Justin tell of some of her escapades in Baton Rouge at the largest high school in the city. These local girls could not imagine what it would be like to attend a school with a thousand students, as both Marion and Linville schools were so small. Justin loved to entertain, and those new friends loved to be entertained by her, especially some of the boys, but she was committed to Larry, and she never dated any of them during her time in north Louisiana.

Justin really loved her time in Linville, but there were moments when she missed the excitement of Baton Rouge, where there were so many opportunities to enjoy other things that simply were not available in rural north Louisiana. This may have been part of the reason for Justin becoming more in love with Larry, but at any rate, things were really heating up between the two, and this eventually led them to intimate moments that overwhelmed them, and they succumbed to their desires. They entered into a deeper relationship because of this, and they begin to hint at the possibility of marriage at some point in the future.

Aunt Pearl began to suspect that Justin and Larry were getting a little bit too serious about one another, and of course, she knew about the dangers in this situation. She secretly worried about the possibility that Justin and Larry may even have been planning to elope, but she worried more that Justin may become pregnant, and in no way did she want to have to tell Justin's grandmother that she had failed in her duties of keeping Justin on a path that would lead to college and the brighter future that Justin's mother and grandmother wanted for their wayward child.

Armond Love told me many years later as we discussed the relationship between Larry and Justin that he remembered seeing them together, along with some other teenagers from school, at the Hooker Hole on the river, and he said that when they touched one another, you could see and feel their love for one another. He said it was so obvious that all of their friends would agree that the bond between these two was really something special.

There were varied opinions with those in the Linville area as to what would come next, and they soon learned of the decision by Uncle Sidney and Aunt Pearl to send Justin back to her grandmother in Baton Rouge. Some thought that Aunt Pearl just simply tired of trying to hold such a spirited young lady in check, while others more familiar with the romance between Justin and Larry assumed that Aunt Pearl was afraid that the two of them were planning to marry; and this she did not want. So she sent Justin south to prevent the marriage. Regardless of whatever reasons may have led to Justin having to leave Linville, it happened, and the aftermath of the separation would lead to a story that would play out over the next sixteen months that would never be forgotten by many of Justin and Larry's friends. I was one of Larry's best friends after he and Justin were separated, and the heartbreak that Larry suffered was something that I witnessed as time passed. The story has been a constant companion of mine for so many long years, and I have known for a long time now that I must tell this story I saw develop after Justin went away. My interest in the story and my concern for Larry grew as I watched, as did his other friends, and several of them shared their observations with me over time.

CHAPTER 4

Spring of 1961

THOSE CLOSEST TO Larry began to see the changes in him during the first few weeks after Justin Cooper left Linville and returned to live with her Grandmother and her sister Grace Marie in Baton Rouge, Louisiana. Larry's mother had to almost drag him out of bed each morning during the school week, and some days he did not get up in time to catch the school bus. On these days he would help his father, Clint, in the chicken houses, and he would feed and water the hogs, then clean up around the small farm, maybe helping in the garden.

In the afternoons on the days Larry missed school, he would bathe and put on clean clothes and drive out to Haile, where he would sit on a bench in front of one of the small stores, where he would meet some of the boys as they got off the school bus there. There would be small talk about what went on at school that day while they drank cokes and ate candy bars while just watching what little traffic came by on the highway. Usually the train would come through on the tracks that paralleled the state highway on the east side all the way to Spencer, where it veered off to the right into the woods until it crossed the river at Sterlington. The Missouri Pacific train would be pulling cars loaded with lumber from the saw mill located in Huttig, Arkansas, as it rolled on to Monroe, Louisiana, where the cars would be routed in various directions from there.

His friends noticed that Larry just stared across the highway most of the time, seeming to have something on his mind, but not sharing it with any of them. Little did they know that he was in the early stages of heartbreak because of Justin's leaving just when they had become totally in love with each other. None of them saw the signs that Larry was depressed, and they seldom heard that funny little laugh that was Larry's trademark.

Baseball season was almost over for the high schools in the area, and on days when we had home games at Linville, I would catch a ride with someone to Haile, and from there I would hitch-hike or walk the five miles home before darkness fell. I remember on one of these occasions, I still had my Hornets baseball uniform and cap on when I caught a ride from school and was dropped off at Thomas' Grocery, where Billy Hill and Larry were sitting on the bread box under the store front, shooting the breeze. The "bread box" was a wooden box, painted red, with a thin sheet metal cover on the hinged top, and it was about thirty inches wide and little over two feet deep and also a little over two feet front to back. These boxes were placed in front of most of the small country stores by the Holsum Bread Company in Monroe, and before daybreak each morning Monday through Friday, their delivery truck would drop off the store's order for light bread (only white enriched sandwich bread was available for purchase in those days), plus honey buns, which the store owners would transfer inside after opening for business each morning. These boxes were sturdy, with short legs underneath to prevent blowing rain from getting up into the box, and they were used more for seating under the storefront, in addition to the always present wooden bench on the opposite side of the front door.

Billy and Larry knew I was hoping for a ride home, so Billy said to me, "come go with us, and I will take you home after we get through riding around".

Billy was several years older than me, and he drove a 1950 model Ford convertible, maroon in color, and since most of the roads leading away from the main highway at that time were dirt roads, the back seat of the car was usually so dusty that your clothes would get extremely dirty if you rode in the back. Most cars in those days were prone to "suck dust", a phrase that most people used to describe what happened to the interior of cars and pickup trucks that drove on the dirt roads in those days. Most vehicles did not have air conditioning and during the hot, dry summer, the windows would be rolled down in order to enjoy what little cooling effect the breeze created while driving along. When two vehicles met on the dusty roads, the clouds of dust they created would cause the breeze to carry the dust into the passing vehicles, where it stuck to the seats and all the exposed surfaces inside of the vehicle. If the inside of your car or pickup was not cleaned regularly, the dust could continue to build up, especially in the back seat of a car.

I readily agreed to go with the Billy and Larry, even though you never knew what you might get into with them. And sure enough, Billy, with a wry grin, told me we were just going for a little ride, and he would get me home pretty soon. He was driving south from Haile, and I knew he was probably going to Perryville or Monroe, as they were the nearest places you could go to buy beer or liquor south of Haile, because they were in adjoining parishes, and due to the fact that sale of alcohol in Union Parish was banned. The only other choice to obtain liquor locally would be a bootlegger who illegally sold briar patch whiskey. Briar patch whiskey was what most locals called the illicit whiskey made by moonshiners, who hid their stills in briar patches many times, in hopes that the local law would not find their still.

Billy Hill was a roughneck who worked for the local drilling companies that drilled for natural gas in what was known as the Monroe Gas Field, an area in northeast Louisiana where natural gas was discovered in the 1920's in the "Monroe Rock", a name given to the porous rock formation that held the natural gas pockets located just over two thousand feet deep in this area. Billy had a dry sense of humor and he would tell stories from time to time that were pretty entertaining.

This day, as Billy was driving down the highway, he began telling me about letting another teenager named Kent Shadic drive his car. Kent was a tall young man who was a cousin of mine, about three years older than me, and like me, he had to walk or hitch-hike, or catch rides wherever he could in order to get around.

Billy told me, "Freddy Ray, let me tell you about Kent Shadic trying to drive my car. He asked me if I would teach him how to drive a couple of weeks ago, and I told him I would. So I let him get behind the wheel while I sat in the shotgun seat (passenger side), and I told him to put the gearshift in neutral, turn on the key, and push the starter button while pressing down a little on the accelerator, and he did real good at that. Then I told him to put his left foot on the clutch, and I showed him where first, second and third gears were located on the gear shift."

Billy continued the story as he drove south toward Sterlington, and he had gotten tickled soon after beginning the tale. "Now, we were on that gravel road that goes down to the Hooker Hole on the river, where there wasn't any traffic, so nobody would get hurt, and the ditches were shallow so hopefully, he wouldn't tear up my little convertible. I told Kent to put the gearshift in low gear, press down on the accelerator a little while still holding the clutch down with his left foot, then to ease out on the clutch until the car started moving. And I told him once it started moving, give it a little gas and I'll tell you when to push the clutch back in and shift it into second gear".

"Kent told me O.K., and he gassed it a little too much and let out on the clutch until the car moved just a little and then he took his foot completely off the clutch so quick that the car took a big leap forward, sputtered and jumped about two more times and he let off on the accelerator, and the motor died, and the car shuddered to a stop."

Billy snickered then and with a slow drawl to emphasize what happened next, he said, "I crawled back over into the front seat from in the back because that first jump was so big, it threw me over in the back seat." Billy laughed again and said, "I told him, I said, now Kent, you need to eeeeaaaase out on that clutch and when the car starts moving, then just give it a little gas kinda slow-like. O.K.?"

Billy continued telling the story, saying that the exact same thing happened a couple more times before he told Kent that he needed to wait a while before trying to drive again. Larry and I knew Billy was exaggerating when he said that the leaping of the car threw him over into the back seat, but we all had a good laugh about it. And I could sympathize with Kent, because I thought about the time when I was about seven years old and my father, who was drunk at the time, made me try to drive for the first time in his old truck with the standard transmission. I went through the leaping and jumping of the truck, and then shuddering to an abrupt halt when the engine died. But I finally got the truck moving, only to get stuck in the deep tracks that cars and trucks had cut into the muddy road. The main reason for my loss of control of the old truck was because of the slack in the steering wheel. The high mileage on the truck caused the steering to be loose, resulting in almost two rounds of slack in the steering wheel before the steering would change directions which caused much difficulty in driving of the vehicle. This slack in the steering caused me to lose control of the truck and get stuck crossways in the middle of the muddy road, and this in turn resulted in a severe scolding for me.

When we went through Sterlington and Billy turned south at the highway intersection just beyond the little town, I knew he was going to Monroe instead of just going to the liquor store at Perryville to get some beer, and I was beginning to regret accepting his offer for the ride. But I was always up for an adventure, especially with my older friends, so I didn't dwell on that any more.

Billy drove on through Monroe and continued south bound on Highway 15, so I didn't have a clue as to where we were going. "Where are we going?" I asked Billy.

"There is a joint about eight or ten miles from here that has a poker room in the back of the building that only a few people know about, because gambling is against the law. I don't mind breaking the law just a little bit, if I can make a few dollars."

"I see," I said. "I'll have to stay in the car because I'm not old enough to go in a beer joint."

"No," replied Billy. "You can go in and sit at the bar and drink a coke and eat some potato chips, and nobody is going to say anything."

"Good," I said, "because I'm getting a little bit hungry."

We turned to the right off the highway into the parking lot of the first building I had seen for what seemed like several miles, after driving through what looked as if it were a swamp. The name of the place was *The Forrest Club*, and it was a pretty big building, with only a couple of cars parked in front, and one other car on the left side of the building where Billy parked. Upon entering the front door, I saw there was a bar with barstools along it on the right side of a huge room, and a few scattered tables in the left side of the room. There was an open area in the left back corner of the room, a dance floor with enough room against the back wall for a band, and I assumed there would be a band playing there on the weekends. A single door was in the middle of the back wall, and it was closed. Billy purchased a beer from the bartender and after taking a couple of sips from the bottle, he leaned over the bar and talked in a low voice to the bartender for a moment, and then he and Larry walked to the back of the room and disappeared through the doorway and they closed the door behind them.

The bartender was an older man who needed a shave, and looked to be someone who needed to get more sunlight on his pasty skin, and he also appeared to be someone who had done very little physical labor in his lifetime. He placed a bottle of coca cola and a package of chips on the bar in front of me. "Your buddy bought these for you," he said. "Where do you play baseball?"

"Linville High School in Linville," I answered. "It's in Union Parish, a few miles south of Marion."

"Yeah, I know where Marion is," he said. "What position do you play?"

I told him I pitched, and that we only scored a couple of runs, but the other team didn't score any runs.

"Oh, you pitched a shutout, huh?" You must be a pretty good pitcher.

"Yes Sir, I guess I am. I've got a real good curve ball, and I can't throw real hard, but I've got good control. Our catcher can read the batter's weaknesses pretty quick, and he will give me a target to throw my fast ball to, like if a batter can't hit a high inside pitch, he will hold his mitt there and I can usually hit it. He is really smart, and that makes me a better pitcher."

"Let me tell you a funny story about the first ball game I pitched," I said. "I pitched one high school game when I was thirteen years old.....in the eighth grade."

"The hell you say!" said the bartender. "The eighth grade?"

"Yes Sir! Mr. Graves was the coach then. That was his last year at Linville, and before baseball season started, he saw me pitching on the school yard, next to the Science Building, which was about eighty feet from the left field line of the baseball field. I was throwing a curve ball to Freddie Platt, and when Mr. Graves saw my curve ball, he told me he was going to give me a uniform and put me on his ball team. I didn't know anything about pitching, and our first game was against Marion, the school six or eight miles north of Linville, and they were our arch rivals. The game was in a tournament at Dubach, and our regular pitcher was Parker Haile, who was a senior and he was a real good pitcher. But Parker had been hurt in a motorcycle wreck and he missed the first three or four ball games that year, so a junior named Johnny Pace started the game as the pitcher. Johnny could throw it a hundred miles an hour, but he didn't know where the ball might go, because he didn't have very good control."

"Yeah, if you can't throw strikes, you can get in trouble real quick," said the bartender as he dragged his barstool down to a point just across the bar from me, and he sat on the stool.

"Well, Johnny threw eight straight balls and none of them were even close to the plate, so Mr. Graves called time out and told me to come to the mound. Mr. Graves told the shortstop to go to the outfield to replace one of the outfielders, and told Johnny to play shortstop. Then he told me to warm up, and he watched as I threw a few pitches, and as he started to walk off the field, he told me to hold the two runners on base. Well, I didn't know a thing about pitching because I had never played in a real ball game before, so I just reared back and started throwing the ball, and on the first pitch the boy on second base stole third! I don't know why the boy on first base didn't steal second, but Mr. Graves called time out and came out to the mound."

"Freddy, you got to pitch out of the stretch when men are on base," he said.

"What's that?" I asked.

Mr. Graves stood with his right foot against the rubber, standing sideways, and he said, "You pitch from this position when men are on base," and he showed me how to wind up, check the runner, and then start the throw toward home plate. "Hold that runner on first! Don't let him steal!" he said, and then he walked off the field.

On my next pitch, I was already beginning my pitch when I caught a glimpse of the boy on first making a break, so I shut her down and threw the ball to first base."

The umpire behind the plate yelled "Balk!" and when he motioned the runner to go to second, I saw him trotting down to second base and I wondered what in the world was going on!

"Time out!" called Mr. Graves, and as he walked out to the mound, he said, "Freddy, once you make that move toward home, you can't throw it to first base!"

"I don't understand," I told him. "I was embarrassed and I know he had to be, because I didn't know anything about baseball, and nothing about pitching for sure, except for trying to throw the baseball by the batter!"

"Then Mr. Graves got up on the mound again and he went through the motions of throwing a pitch, and he showed me at what point I had to go on with my pitch, so I wouldn't balk. I was dumb, but I was smart enough to know I ought to be embarrassed, but I got back up on the mound and kept pitching out of the stretch. The first batter I pitched to hit a ground ball and was thrown out at first base, and then this big tall batter, Bill Brashier, the cleanup hitter who I knew was all district in baseball and basketball, came up to the plate, and I was scared to death! But somehow, I struck him out, and I don't remember anything else about that game except that we won it, one to nothing! I don't know how we did it, but we did! You see, my curve ball was pretty fast, and it would go toward the plate straight for a long ways, then it would break big time! I could throw a pretty hard fast ball for a thirteen year old, and with my good control, I guess that was how we won that game!"

"Wow!" said the bartender. "I wish I could have seen that game!"

"But you know, the next day, Mr. Graves told me that the Marion coach asked him how old I was after that game, and when Mr. Graves told him I was thirteen, he said that coach told him that I was too young to play high school baseball, and he was going to report Mr. Graves to the Louisiana Athletic Commission if he didn't take my uniform away from me. And he did take it! So that wound up my high school baseball until the tenth grade!"

The bartender slowly shook his head. "He must have been a sore loser," he said.

"He was a real good coach, and he hates to lose so bad," I said. "Especially to Linville! And I wound up pitching for him in Dixie Youth baseball the summer just before I turned fifteen. Every time I pitched a shutout, he would give me a brand new baseball, still in the box, and I still have four or five of them! So I don't feel bad at all about him getting me kicked off the team that time."

"Well, that's good," he said. "I didn't play ball when I was in school, because I quit school when I was fifteen." Then he walked past the cash register and sat down in a chair behind the bar near the front door, where he reached for a small paperback western book by the cash register and began reading.

I sat there for about forty five minutes, during which time a young man who appeared to be about thirty years of age came in and sat a few barstools down from me. He said howdy to me as he sat down, and never spoke again as he sat there drinking one beer, then ordering another as he stared across the bar at the bottles of liquor on a shelf near the cash register.

Billy came back into the bar and ordered another beer. "We'll be out in a few minutes," he said. "I know you're probably ready to head for the hills." He grinned as he looked back at me as he walked toward the back room.

I got up from the barstool, stretched, and walked out the front door, then stumbled through the oversized gravel in the parking lot to the corner of the building. I waited for Billy and Larry just around the corner of the building for a few minutes until I heard the front door open and close.

I could hear the crunching of boots in the gravel and heard someone talking, so I assumed it was Billy and Larry coming toward the corner of the building. I eased up close to the corner, and just before they got to the corner, I jumped out with my right arm back, fist clinched as if I were going to hit someone, and I yelled, "you son-of-a…..", but to my surprise, It was the guy who had been sitting by himself at the bar when I walked out.

He threw both arms up in front of his face and shouted "Oh no", while backpedaling to keep from getting hit with a fist.

Thinking the talking was one of my buddies talking to the other, instead of this guy talking out loud to himself, I had tried to play a joke on my friends, but I was shocked and surprised more than this guy was, or more than Billy and Larry would have been.

I immediately began apologizing to the guy I had feigned hitting, telling him, "I'm sorry…..I thought you were my friends and I was just going to mess with them! I didn't know it was you. I'm sorry!"

"That's alright," he said. "Boy, I thought I was about to get busted in the nose. Man, you sure scared me!" He laughed and told me, "That'll teach me not to be talking to myself from now on!"

I laughed with him and apologized again, and he walked on just as the door opened as Billy and Larry walked out.

As we got in Billy's car, I told them about scaring the guy who was driving out of the parking lot. They laughed and Larry told me, "Boy, you're lucky he didn't turn you ever which way but loose!"

"Yeah, I know. You can bet I'll never try to play that trick on anybody else. That fellow was big enough, he could have killed me. But he was so glad it was just a joke, he was happy to just walk away. And I'm glad!"

It seemed as if it took twice as long to drive back to Haile as it took to get to the Forrest Club originally, and there was little talk from any of us during the trip.

As we were nearing Haile, Larry began telling us how much he missed Justin Cooper, and that he knew she wanted to stay in school at Linville, and graduate there.

"Her Aunt Pearl thought we were going to get married," he said. "And I think that she thought that I wasn't good enough for Justin. We hadn't really talked about it much, but I would have married her in a minute. Boy, she is beautiful, wild as she can be, and so much fun. I sure do wish she could have stayed here."

That was the first time I had heard Larry speak of Justin, and I could feel a sense of sadness in his voice that touched me. This night would be the beginning of my witnessing Larry's growing realization of the magnitude of his love for Justin, and his loss of her companionship that would consume him as time marched on.

We dropped him off at his house before Billy drove the five miles from Haile to my home, and we talked about Larry's comments, but I don't think either of us could have predicted then where Larry's love and loss would take him in the future.

Billy apologized for taking so long to get me home as he pulled up in front of our place, and I got out of the car, shut the door and leaned over and stuck my head inside the open window on the passenger side of the car. I thanked him and told him that it was fine.......I had enjoyed the trip.

"You're welcome," said Billy, "I'll see you around in a few days." I backed away from the car and Billy revved up the engine and pulled out onto the graveled road, the car tires making a loud crunching noise in the gravel as he drove away.

As I opened the gate leading into our yard, stepped through, and closed it behind me, I thought about the lonesome sound of Larry's voice as he had talked about Justin Cooper. Little did I know that night that this was to be the beginning of a story about heartbreak that I would witness during the year following Justin's departure from Linville.

The rest of the story is one that I carry with me to this day, one that I have wanted to put into writing for several decades now. A year ago, my wife, Diane, and I purchased new furniture for our office in our home, and as we were sorting through papers accumulated over many years, throwing away that which we no longer needed or wanted, Diane found two folded sheets of legal sized copy paper, yellowed with age, and she asked me, "What is this?"

I unfolded the sheets of paper, and there was the handwritten beginning of my story about my friend, Larry Scarborough. The yellowing of the paper with age made me realize how long ago it had been since I first wanted to tell this story, and it brought tears to my eyes.

"This is the beginning of Larry's story," I said. "This yellowed paper shows how long ago I was thinking about doing this story! I was going to write it as fiction, but not knowing where Justin was, I realized I could not complete the story without talking with her, and also it would have to be true to what actually happened."

CHAPTER 5

Early Summer, 1961

SHORTLY BEFORE THE school year ended, Larry had taken a bottle of India ink used in the mimeograph machine in the school library, where the school newspaper was printed, and he began using the ink to do crude tattoos on some of the boys he ran with, and since I was beginning my time as a teenage rebel, I decided I would let him tattoo my middle name on my right arm. We made plans to meet at the Brown Brothers Grocery one Saturday in early June, and there he would do the tattoo for me.

I walked almost four miles toward Haile that Saturday afternoon before someone came along and picked me up as I hitch-hiked and dropped me off in Haile, where I waited for Larry as I sat in front of Brown Brothers grocery store. I didn't have to wait long for Larry, who drove up in his 1956 black and orange Oldsmobile, and he carried a small paper bag as he got out of his car and came up under the storefront. "Are you ready to get stuck?" Larry asked as I stood up from the old worn wooden bench I had been sitting on.

"Yeah, I guess so," I replied. "You're not gonna hurt me too bad, are you?"

"You're tough. I think you'll survive," Larry said, and then came his trademark giggle/laugh. "Come on in the store where we can sit down while I do your tattoo."

47

Larry pointed at a chair near the center of the store, close to the tall natural gas space heater. "Sit in that chair, with the arms on it, so you can rest your arm there and I can do my artwork," and he laughed again. "I'll sit on that apple crate."

I did as I was instructed, and Larry moved the wooden apple crate over to the right side of my chair and sat down on it as he reached into the paper bag and removed a small bottle of ink, a spool of white sewing thread with one of his mother's sewing needles that was stuck into the side of the spool of thread. "Jim Ollie, can I borrow an ink pen for a minute?" he asked the Brown brother who normally ran the store. Jim Ollie's brother, Ferris, was usually busy taking care of his post office duties in the small room that served as the post office in the back corner of the building, or he was either taking care of the books for the store.

"Yeah," said Jim Ollie, as he reached for the pen in his shirt pocket and handed it to Larry. "What you going to do?" he asked.

"I'm gonna put a tattoo on Freddy Ray's arm."

Jim Ollie just shook his head from side to side slowly two or three times, with a disapproving expression on his face, then he walked to the far side of the store and began moving some of the store items around slightly, aligning them to be displayed in a more orderly fashion.

Larry positioned my right arm as he wanted on the chair's arm, and then he took the pen and slowly wrote *R a y* across the middle of my upper arm. He pulled the needle out of the spool of thread and he began to wrap the thread around the point of the needle until he had a small ball of thread on the end of the needle, the ball of thread being almost a quarter of an inch in diameter. He pulled on the thread from the spool to break it and then he made a loop and tied it around the ball on the point of the needle. He took the cap off the bottle of ink and stuck the needle down into the bottle far enough to submerge the end with the ball of thread, held it for a few seconds over the bottle until the ink stopped dripping, and then he grabbed my arm just above the elbow with his left hand, pulling it out toward him. "Here we go!" he said as he leaned his head close to my arm, and then he began to stick the needle into my arm with a quick jabbing motion beginning at the top of the R.

"Ohhh, that hurts," I said as I winced and tried to pull my arm away, but Larry held tightly to my arm to keep me from pulling away.

"I told you it was gonna hurt a little!" he said with a grin on his face. "I'm gonna stick you about a thousand more times before this is over!"

"Well, be as gentle as you can," I said as my eyes moistened a bit. But as Larry continued dipping into the ink and resuming the writing on my arm, there would be every few seconds, as he was sticking the needle into my arm, a deeper thrust with the needle that was really painful. Those deeper pricks with the needle would cause me to express my pain more than usual, and that would bring a reaction from Jim Ollie Brown.

"Hell, that's what you wanted!" Jim Ollie snapped at me. "You wanted it, so quit your damned whining and crying!"

So I clenched my teeth together and just grunted softly when the needle went too deep after that, mad at Jim Ollie for scolding me. I had heard 'The truth hurts' before.....it was what I wanted, but I still didn't like Jim Ollie talking to me that way. I could tell that he knew I was doing something I would regret later in life. And this was true, because when Larry completed the tattoo, I stood up and looked down at the name tattooed on my arm, instead of it being near level across my arm, it was on a downward slope from the R to the Y, so in addition to having a crude, home-made tattoo on my arm, it was nowhere near level. My mother and grandmother were not too proud of me when they saw it, but the tattoo stayed with me through my rebel years, and after I was out of school and working for a living, I had a doctor cut it out of my arm. I was given a local to prevent the pain during the surgery, but below the incision to hull the ink out of my arm, I could feel the blood running down my arm before the nurse wiped it away each time before it reached my elbow. After that experience, I likened it to be as if Larry and I were blood brothers, but it was only my blood. That was not the first bad decision I had made as a teenager, but somewhere in the middle of a long line of such moves.

CHAPTER 6

— ❧ —

Summer, 1961

WHEN THE SCHOOL year ended in May, Larry decided that he would not return to Linville High in the fall. I don't know for sure the reasons for his decision, but I'm sure that since Justin was back in Baton Rouge, he simply did not want to be there. He had grown tired of working in his Dad's chicken houses, so he began looking for work to earn money to pay for gasoline and for maintenance of his car, and he soon found one in Marion at the Allen Brothers Hatchery.

The hatchery furnished baby chicks to the local chicken farmers, and at that time, there were not a lot of chicken farmers in the area, and most of them only had one small chicken house. Clint Scarborough had one house that held six thousand chickens and two that were a bit smaller where they raised five thousand chickens per house during each cycle. These were typical houses at the time, and it would take fourteen to sixteen weeks for the chickens to be fully grown and ready to be picked up by Allen Brother's trucks of Marion, Louisiana, for transport to a facility where they would be processed. The feeding and watering of the chickens was all done by hand, making the process labor intensive.

Today, chicken farmers may have a half dozen or more monstrous houses where the feeding and watering is done automatically with state of the art equipment, and a chicken house may cost as much as five hundred thousand dollars in construction and equipment costs. In these huge houses, as many as forty thousand chickens are brought to the desired weight of approximately six and one half pounds each in seven weeks, with several hundred thousand pounds of feed being used during this period, plus as much as three thousand gallons of water per day consumed by the flock as they reach maturity.

Larry had started drinking more beer after Justin had left Linville, but the Allen family that owned the hatchery knew he was a good, dependable worker, who had shouldered most of the work load in his family's chicken houses, so the Allen family hired him soon after he applied for work there. I, for one, appreciated the fact that they hired Larry after finding out that he did not intend to complete his final year of high school, and since there were few secrets in the area, I was sure they had heard that he had been drinking quite a bit.

Almost every Saturday afternoon during that summer, I would walk or hitch-hike out to Haile and meet up with the older boys and we would usually ride around in the countryside and drink beer and smoke cigarettes, listening to music on the car radio of Larry's car, or Billy Hill's 1950 Ford convertible, or in an ever changing mix of old cars or pickups. I would give a couple of dollars or whatever I had to help pay for the beer and gasoline whenever I had money. My grandmother drew a sixty dollar old age pension from the state, and she only bought her blood pressure medicine from this money, the rest going to the six younger boys in our family, or to our sister, Myra. My father very seldom gave us any spending money, and he never seemed concerned about where I was going or what I would be doing when I left home. I was the only one of the brothers, it seemed, to be born with the wanderlust, and the rebel ways that kept me in trouble.....nothing bad.....just mischievous behavior.

Larry Scarborough was almost always in the mix when we gathered up on the weekend, and there was Sugarboy McKinnie, Billy Tom Ellis, Don Jenny, Billy Hill, Sidney Ray, Jerry Colson, along with others who drifted in and out of the group who hung around Haile and passed the time entertaining one another. We all drank beer, but not in excess, because we really could not afford that much, since we usually pooled our money to send with someone who would be going outside the parish to buy beer.

Larry's dad, Clint Scarborough, allowed Larry to make some homebrew beer that summer, and he told him how it to brew it and bottle it. His only mistake in making this beer was not having enough beer bottles to bottle all of his beer, so Larry bottled some of it in Mason jars that his mother, Myrt, normally used for canning vegetables.

I think Larry actually bottled his beer before it was completely fermented. This, in addition to storing the bottled beer in a small storage building in the back yard where the heat inside of the building would be above 100 degrees on most summer afternoons, would lead to some of the Mason jars of beer exploding from time to time.

Larry picked me up from Haile one hot afternoon, and we rode back to his house, because he just wanted to visit and he also wanted to show me how much beer he had bottled. When we arrived there, his dad was sitting in a cane bottomed straight back chair under a shade tree beside the house. Because few people had air conditioned homes at that time, it was usually more pleasant to sit under a shade tree where you would get an occasional breeze blowing through, making it cooler than being indoors. Larry and I pulled chairs up closer to where his dad was sitting and we sat and talked about the heat and work for a little while. Our conversation was interrupted by the sound of a muffled explosion coming from behind the house. Larry jumped up and looked toward the storage building where his beer was stored. "There goes another bottle of my beer," he said as he laughed and began walking in the direction of the building.

Clint frowned and said to Larry as he walked away, "I told you that you couldn't bottle beer in fruit jars!"

Larry was opening the door to the storage building when I walked up to it, and as I looked inside and saw the shattered glass everywhere, I told him, "It looks like a bomb went off in here!"

And there was that funny laugh from Larry. "I know it! It has been about ten days since I bottled the beer, and for the first week, we didn't have any jars explode. But in the last three or four days, we have had one or two jars explode every day! None of the beer bottles have exploded, but these jars have thinner glass, and they are little bombs! Daddy told me the beer is still brewing, so we better start drinking it or we won't have any left to drink if this keeps happening!'

I backed away from the door of the building, because I was afraid another jar would explode and I might get splintered glass in my eyes. I agreed with Larry. "Why don't we go to Haile and get some ice and ice down some of the beer that's in the beer bottles?"

"Let's do it," said Larry. "I'll call Billy George and tell him we are gonna have a beer drinking good time tonight! He needs to come to Haile and get in on it!"

Larry had an ice chest in the trunk of his car, so he and I rode out to Brown Brothers' Grocery and paid for a ten pound block of ice before going around to the side of the building to the little insulated ice house. While Larry brought the ice chest from the car, I took the ice tongs that lay on the short wooden deck attached to the front of the ice house, opened the door and stuck the tongs inside, spreading them out to grab the block of ice. When Larry sat the ice chest on the ground in front of the ice house, I placed the block of ice into the chest and Larry pulled his pocket knife from the pocket of his jeans, opened the long blade and began chopping the block of ice into fist sized pieces. Once this was done, we drove back to the Scarborough home so we could put some of the beer on ice, picking several sixteen ounce beer bottles and one quart sized beer bottle to put into the ice chest.

After Larry called Billy George, he and I rode back to the Hooker Hole Road and turned left toward Dewey Roberson's house. We stopped to pick up Don Jenny, who was staying with his sister and Dewey, his brother-in-law, for a few days. They lived only about a quarter of a mile south of Larry's home, alongside the river road.

When we left there, Larry drove a mile or so toward the river, then pulled off onto a pipeline and stopped the car a short distance from the road. He reached into the glove box of his car and pulled out a 'church key', he called it.....a beer opener with a pointed opener that curved downward on one end for opening cans, and on the other end the tip was square for opening bottles. "Let's see how a cold home brew tastes," he said as he smiled and stepped out of the car. He walked to the rear of the car and opened the trunk before retrieving a bottle of beer from the ice chest.

We stood around the car after Larry opened the beer and we passed it around, each one of us taking a sip and passing it to the next one until the bottle was empty. We all agreed that it was a lot stronger than the canned beer bought from the liquor stores, and we assumed that it probably had a lot more kick to it.

Larry had his car radio playing, and as we were drinking the beer, *The Wanderer* by Dion and the Belmonts was played, then *Hello Mary Lou* by Ricky Nelson, and then *Hats Off to Larry* by Del Shannon as he sang '*Hats off to Larry, he broke your heart, just like you broke mine when you said we must part*'. Don and I kidded Larry about that song.......'Ole Larry, the heartbreaker," Don said, and I agreed with him.

"Man, I ain't no heartbreaker," said Larry. "I'm heartbroke!"

There was silence for a minute or two after that, and I thought about Justin leaving, and to myself I said, "He's telling the truth.....he is heartbroken!"

It was then Ray Charles' recording of *Hit The Road Jack* came blaring from the radio, and Larry said, "that's what we'd better do, or else we'll get into that beer and there won't be any left by the time we get back to Haile, and Billy George won't be too happy with us about that!"

The sun was going down as we arrived back at Browns' store, and there Billy George sat on the bench out front, along with Billy Tom Ellis. The door glasses were down on Larry's car and he pulled around to the side of the store and yelled at them to come get in the car with us. As they walked up to Larry's car, Billy Tom pointed toward his 1950 Ford car near the back side of the store and told Larry, "let me get my cigarettes and car keys and I'll be right with y'all."

After the two others got into the car with us, Larry pulled away from the store and drove back down to the river road, and he proceeded to drive down to the dam on the south end of Finch Lake. We just sat in the car and shared a couple more bottles of the home brew, talking and smoking as darkness fell, listening to the radio, and finally rolling the car windows up because the cigarette smoke was not enough to keep the mosquitoes out of the car after sundown.

I recall us listening to Webb Pierce's song, *I Ain't Never*, as darkness was falling. The radio had been turned down low, but Larry turned the volume up when Webb started the song. "We got to listen to Webb, because he's from West Monroe," Larry said.

The others talked about the stout beer, girls and cars, as I sat quietly in the back seat, trying to listen to the songs on the radio and the conversation at the same time. The early sixties was such a special time for music, when country, Motown, rock & roll, R&B and popular music were all played on the same radio station. My favorite song at the time drew my attention completely away from the conversation when it came on, Del Shannon's 'Run-away'.

After a while, we were down to one bottle of beer, and that was the quart of beer, so we decided to take a little break from the beer and ride around a while. We rode on down the graveled road to the Hooker Hole landing on the river, and we sat there a little while looking at the shine of the ripples in the water in the light from the sliver of the moon that had appeared above the treetops across the river. I have always loved the peaceful feeling you get from a scene such as that. There was very little conversation after we had been there for thirty minutes or so, and Larry started the car, pulled out to the road and drove slowly back toward Haile.

When we reached the end of the graveled road where the blacktop began, just a quarter mile from the road that would lead to Larry's home, he slowed the car down to a crawl and after we passed his road and approached a bridge over a small creek a hundred yards from there, Larry pulled the car over to the side of the narrow roadway, cut the engine, opened his car door and stepped out.

"Well, we got one big old bottle of beer left, so why don't we just sit in a circle and pass it around, and when it's gone, we'll load up and go home," said Larry, and we all piled out of the car, agreeing that this sounded like a good idea.

After getting the quart of beer out of the ice chest in the trunk of the car, Larry unscrewed the top from the bottle, and the five of us formed a circle in the middle of the road, then we sat down on our butts in the road and crossed our feet. We passed the bottle from one to the other, sipping from it until it was empty. It didn't take that long, but we did not rush to finish the beer, because at night, there was hardly ever any traffic on that road, so we just simply enjoyed our time together in the dim light, creating a memory. No one talked as we passed the bottle around the circle, which in a way, reminded me of a scene in a western I had seen on television, that being of Indians sitting on the ground in the same fashion, passing the peace pipe around. After we emptied the bottle of beer, we all agreed that, of the popular brands of beer we had tasted before, the worst of them tasted a lot better than Larry's home brew.

We got up from our sitting positions and stretched, a couple of us lit cigarettes, then piled back into the car and Larry drove to Haile, where Billy George got into his car to go home, Billy Tom and I got into his car and he took me home, and Larry took Don back to his sister's house. I don't think any one of us ever tasted another drop of home brewed beer after that night, and this was a good thing!

LARRY
SCARBOROUGH

BILLY McKINNIE

BILLY TOM ELLIS

BOBBIE
ROBERSON

DON
JENNY

CHAPTER 7

Challenge & Trade

A COUPLE OF weeks after our session with the home brew beer, Larry, Billy George, and Sidney Ray showed up at about the same time at Ed Thomas' Grocery in Haile. After exchanging small talk on the store front, they walked inside and said hello to the storekeeper, Ed Thomas, and to a customer, Ferris Ray Brown. Ferris Ray was the younger of two sons of Ferris Brown, Postmaster and co-owner of the store next door. Ed Thomas was a handsome young man, married, and he and his wife had two young children. He was a man with lots of energy, a good personality, and he had developed a good business in his store. In addition to groceries, he stocked shirts, jeans, and shoes for men, plus he carried feed for farm animals in the back of the building, and he also had gasoline pumps in front of the building, as did most rural grocery stores during that time.

On this particular day, he had eight or ten eggs laying on the counter beside his cash register, and Ferris Ray asked why he had those eggs there, instead of in an egg carton.

"They have some small cracks in the shells, and I can't sell them," said Ed, "but let me tell you what I will do. I will let you take these eggs....I'll put them in a little paper bag for you, and we will go outside. You give me about a twenty foot running start, and you can throw those eggs at me, and

I'll give you a quarter for every egg you hit me with. But you will have to give me a dime for every one you miss me with."

Ferris Ray laughed at the proposal, but he said, "O. K., you've got yourself a deal!" He counted nine eggs, and thought about it for a moment. "If I hit you with three eggs, I will come out ahead, so let's do it!"

With that, Ed reached under the counter for a small paper bag, and as the other boys stood there grinning, he placed the eggs in the bag and handed it to Ferris Ray. "Let's go, big boy," he said as he came from behind the counter and headed toward the front door, and out to the graveled parking area to the left of the store.

"I hope I don't mess your clothes up too bad," said Ferris Ray, laughing as he began to turn the top of the paper bag down and roll it further down in order to be able to reach into the bag and get the eggs easier. "Take off," he said, "and you had better run fast!"

"Twenty feet head start now," Ed said as he took a step toward the back of the store. "I'll yell "Go" when I get twenty feet out." And with that, he was off and running, and as soon as he yelled "Go", and Ferris Ray began to run, Ed made a ninety degree turn to the right and an egg sailed behind him and splattered as it hit the gravel.

Ed was running toward the back of the store building, and the few tall, scattered pine trees behind the store, with Ferris Ray in hot pursuit, and behind him ran Larry, Sidney and Billy George, laughing loudly as they tried to keep up in order to see the show. Ferris Ray let fly with another egg that missed Ed just before he disappeared around the back corner of the building. Ed ran toward the first of the pine trees and he ran around the right side of the tree and made a sharp left turn beyond it, and the next egg splattered against the tree. This chase went on through the other trees and then Ed ran toward the other side of the store building, turning left under the store front just before the last egg flew past him. Ed had kept count as the eggs splattered, so he stepped out from the store front and lifted both arms up high, laughing loudly as Ferris Ray stopped, exhausted and grinning, and he shook his head. He was not really the athletic type, and he realized he had been no match for the young storekeeper, who was both fast on his feet and agile.

"Boy, I didn't know you could run so fast!" Ferris Ray told Ed. "Man, I'm give out," breathing hard, and as he walked toward the front of the store where Ed stood, he reached down in his right front pocket, pulling out his change. "The way I got it figured, you just sold them rotten eggs for ninety cents!" he said with a sheepish grin on his face.

"Well, I figured I would make money on this deal, but I really didn't think you would buy every one of them!" said Ed. "That's what I call turning a loss into a profit," he said as Ferris Ray counted out ninety cents and placed it into Ed's hand.

Larry, Billy George and Sidney walked up beside Ferris Ray as he paid Ed, and Larry told him, "you can really throw hard, Ferris Ray, but your aim ain't worth a flip!" and he laughed as he slapped Ferris Ray on his back. "Come on in the store. I'll buy you a coke, because you need something after that workout." And they all walked back into the store.

Ferris Ray got a bottle of Coca Cola out of the coke box near the front door, and Ed waved Larry away as he tried to pay for the coke. "That was worth the cost of the coke to me," said Ed. "That was more fun than I have had in a long time!"

After a few minutes had passed and the laughs were over about the egg chase, Ed told Ferris Ray, "I noticed how you were breathing so hard after chasing me. You should quit smoking those cigarettes. As a matter of fact, all of y'all should quit smoking. Well, Sidney, you don't smoke, do you?"

"No Sir," said Sidney. "I can't afford to buy them."

Ferris Ray looked at Ed, surprised that the storekeeper did not know that he was a non-smoker. "Hey, Mr. Ed, I don't smoke and I never have smoked! I was breathing so hard because I chased you so hard, not because I smoke."

Ed apologized to Ferris Ray then, and he looked at Larry and Billy George with a serious expression on his face. "Let me tell y'all what I will do if you promise me you will quit smoking. You can go right over there and pick out you a shirt....any of them that you want, and I will give you that shirt if you will just promise me right now that you will quit those cigarettes!"

Billy George thought about it for a minute, and then he said, "I don't think I can quit smoking. That sounds like a good deal to me, but I really don't think I can do it!"

Larry was really fond of pretty shirts, so the offer was one that he couldn't turn down. "I'll take you up on that deal if you really mean it," he told Ed.

"I mean it," said Ed as he pointed toward the shirt rack. "Go pick out one and then bring your pack of cigarettes and give them to me."

Larry went over and looked through several of the shirts in his size before picking one. He then did as Ed had instructed, as he walked to the counter, he pulled a half empty pack of cigarettes from his shirt pocket and handed them to Ed. "Thank You," he said. "I appreciate this."

Larry walked out of the store that day convinced that he could quit smoking, but after a few days, he knew that he was too addicted to cigarettes to quit them that easily, and he smoked only a very few each day for a week or so. But soon he was smoking full time, but he never smoked around Ed Thomas again, because he was too ashamed of failing to keep his end of the bargain.

CHAPTER 8

August, 1961

THE SUMMER DAYS drifted by as usual in Louisiana, hot and humid, and the nights were not much better. Larry Scarborough worked Monday through Friday at the hatchery, and he spent his weekends driving around and it seemed someone always had an ice chest with their beer on ice in the trunk of their car or in the bed of their pickup truck. Larry drank some during the week, but on the weekend he, like a number of the older boys around Haile, would drink probably more than he should.

Larry would occasionally date someone else, but it was usually for only one night, because he was not in search of a relationship. Justin Cooper was always on his mind and there would be no changing of that! And the few dates he had with other girls would seem to spur an increase in his drinking in the days following these dates. I assumed this was because he felt guilty for 'cheating' on Justin, even though she was now married to another man and living in Baton Rouge.

There was one particular event that I remember so well that took place in late summer that troubled me quite a bit. Vada Norman owned the third grocery store on the right as you were going south through Haile, and she and her husband had added an extension on the left side of the building for a café and a small frame house on the back of the building. They lived about a half mile from Haile prior to adding the small house on the back of the store and moving into it. It was much more convenient for the family as they spent most of their time minding the store and working in the café. The only problem with the Normans living in the back of the building was the fact that many of the older boys who had cars loved to spin their cars in a circle around a single power pole that stood about half way between the Norman's store and Jordan's Grocery approximately a hundred feet south of Normans. The area between the two stores was graveled and the roaring engines of the cars as they cut this donut around the 'light pole', they called it, and the flying gravel in the middle of the night was highly disturbing to the Normans, who went to bed pretty early because they had to get up early in the mornings to open for business. Over a period of time, the relationship between the local hot rodding beer drinkers and Vada Norman deteriorated to the point of her having to call the Sheriff Department to try to stop the disturbing of her family's peace. At times, teenage boys are not very considerate of others feelings when they are drinking, and some of them, when they know they are aggravating someone, seem to relish the thought of doing so. But everyone, including most of these trouble makers, loved the fact that there was now a café in the little community of Haile, a café that made good hamburgers and French fries, and also had a juke box with the latest hit songs along with the older favorites on it.

I was there during mid-afternoon on this particular Saturday, and I don't remember any of our friends being there, but Larry Scarborough was dropped off at the café by someone, and I did not see who it was, but when he came into the café, it was apparent that he had been drinking pretty heavily. He was a bit unsteady on his feet and his speech was slurred as he sat down on a stool at the counter next to me. He handed me a quarter and asked if I would play the juke box.

"What do you want to hear?" I asked

"I don't care. Play some of that old sad stuff…..beer drinking music…. because I have been drinking beer!"

I walked over to the juke box and as I dropped the quarter in the slot, the clanging sound of the coin dropping into the juke box ended with the click that indicated that it had been accepted. I began looking through the listings, and the first sad song I saw was *I Fall to Pieces* by Patsy Cline, so I punched the number in to play it, and continued looking for the sad ones. I really liked Don Gibson's *Sea of Heartbreak*, so I played it and then I played another of my favorites, Bobby Darin's *Dream Lover*. I stood there several more minutes searching for sad songs until I had selected the total of five songs.

After selecting the songs, I sat down on the stool and asked Larry where he had been, and he told me he had been to the Swayback Bar over past Fairbanks, Louisiana with Sugarboy, and he had him drop him off at the café, so he could sober up some before he went home. He stood up before the second song was finished on the juke box and walked unsteadily over to the door, and he stood there for a minute looking out toward the highway before he opened the door and walked out.

I sat there listening to the music until the last song played, and then I walked outside to check on Larry. He was leaning against the front of the building, still staring across the highway with a blank look on his face as if he were in deep thought. I didn't say anything as I walked just past where he was and I leaned against the wall beside him. He looked toward the door of the café to his left and just beyond the door, a toad frog hopped along and stopped within a foot of the door, where he sat motionless for a moment.

Larry suddenly walked over and picked the frog up, and said to him, "hello, little buddy. What are you doing out here on this hot afternoon? You ought to be parked under a tall weed somewhere……where it's cool!"

Then he took a few steps away from the building and sat down with his butt resting on his heels. He placed the frog down in front of him in the sandy gravel and scattered rocks, and he began to pet him, stroking the frog along his back with his fingers. "You're my little buddy," he said. "I've got to give you a name. I think I'll call you Tommy.....yeah.....Tommy...... Tommy the Toad! Yeah, that's a good name for you, little buddy." Larry had his head down almost between his knees in his squatting position, still petting the frog.

I was still leaning against the café wall, grinning at this seventeen year old, down on the ground, playing with a toad frog, and petting him..... talking to him.....giving him a name, and a pretty good name, I thought. Larry was oblivious of what was going on around him as he played with his new friend. An older man who lived in the area drove up, got out of his car, and walked to the door of the café, looking down at Larry with a quizzical expression on his face as he walked by him. I was a bit embarrassed for Larry's sake as this scene played out before me.

After playing with Tommy the Toad for a few minutes, Larry moved forward a couple of feet to a place where there was more sand. He began scratching out a hole with his hand in the sandy gravel deep enough to put the frog in. He then placed the frog in the hole and began covering him with sand he raked up with some of the small pebbles mixed in the sand. He began patting the sand/pebble mix down pretty firmly as he buried the frog, saying as he pressed down rather firmly, "so long, little buddy."

I walked over to Larry quickly as I told him, "Larry, don't bury that little frog alive! That's mean! I thought he was your buddy!"

"Aww, I ain't burying him.....I'm just playing like it. You know they live in holes in the ground anyway." Then he began to scratch the sand away until he could pick the frog up out of the hole. "There, little Tommy.

Did I scare you? I was just messing with you." Then he brushed the sand off the frog and placed him on the ground beside the hole and began petting him again, not speaking, only stroking his fingers down along the frog's back.

A couple more customers came walking up to the door of the café as Larry continued to play with the frog, and they laughed at him as they passed by. I'm sure they knew him and assumed that he may have had a few too many beers, and once again, I felt embarrassment for Larry, thinking that his heartbreak was really beginning to tell on him. He moved forward until he was on his knees, and then he plopped down in the gravel on his butt and crossed his feet in front of him.

Larry scratched in the sand to make another hole, and he covered the frog once more, being too rough in the process, and I was afraid he was going to kill the frog. I felt it was time for me to get involved at that point, so I bent over and uncovered the frog myself, picked him up, and took him just beyond the corner of the café and placed him in the grass up against the wall. "I was afraid you were gonna kill Tommy, so I saved his life! I bet he won't forget you for a while!" Larry didn't reply as he remained sitting in the gravel, and he dropped his head down, staring at the ground by his feet. I thought he was going to go to sleep in that position.

It was only a few minutes later when Don Jenny drove up in his sister's car, stopping within three or four feet of where Larry was, and he tooted the car horn one short blast. Larry jerked his head up to see who it was, and he laughed that silly little laugh when he saw his friend get out of the car. "What in the world is going on here?" Don asked.

"Larry has been playing with a toad frog," I said. "He named him Tommy, and he's been petting him. Then he buried him a couple of times and I thought he was gonna kill him, so I rescued him and put him in the grass around the corner there," pointing to the corner of the café.

"I think he has had a little too much to drink," I whispered to Don as I stepped forward with my face close to his ear.

"Uh huh," said Don, nodding his head slowly. He extended his right hand down to Larry. "Here Larry, give me your hand and let me help you up."

Larry did as he was instructed and with a grunt, he stood up with Don's help. "You got any beer?"

"No, I don't have any beer. I'm driving Gay's car, and Dewey would throw a fit if I was drinking and driving her car," said Don. "Come on. Go with me and we will ride around a while. We need to talk." He got behind Larry and placed both hands on his shoulders and gently pushed him toward the passenger side of the car, opened the door, and Larry got in. Don slammed the door shut and winked at me as he came around the front of the car and got behind the wheel, started the car and drove away.

I stood there, still a little bewildered by what I had just witnessed. But you never knew what you might see around this little community. "Must be something in the water around here," I thought to myself, and I walked back into the café.

CHAPTER 9

Autumn 1961

BACK IN THE summer when Billy Tom purchased his 1950 Ford coupe, it had lots of miles on it from its previous owners. Billy Tom was so proud of it, you could see it in his attitude, for nothing could ruin his days…he was the owner of his first car, always a huge event in a teenager's life. Shortly after he bought the car, he removed the muffler, and replaced it with a straight exhaust. The car's exhaust was pretty loud, and when Billy Tom took his foot off the accelerator, as the car was slowing down, the car's exhaust would make a loud, rapid popping noise and the popping sounds would seem to get louder and the timing between the popping would be further and further apart as the car kept slowing down. The straight pipe exhaust system was not unusual during that period of time, but you could get a traffic ticket if you created too much noise in town. If you drove to the limit of the speed the car would do in first and second gears, and then let off on the gas without depressing the clutch, the exhaust would make a louder noise as the engine was gearing down. I thought Billy Tom's car was pretty cool, and we rode a lot of miles at night, listening to Randy's Record Mart on a high frequency radio station out of Gallatin, Tennessee, a station which played a lot of blues and R&B music. I loved to hear St. James Infirmary by Bobby Blue Bland, and songs like Cry to Me by Solomon Burke.

As Billy Tom and I were riding around in his new ride one Saturday night in October, we left Haile and decided to go to the Alabama Landing via the Charlie Lee Road, which is now known as Brown Pace Road. This road was graveled until it went beyond a few houses in the first half mile of the road, and then it turned into a narrow dirt road for a few miles, where there was only a couple of houses in the next half mile, and then there was nothing but thick woods on each side of the road until it reached the Alabama Landing Road. I always thought it was a little spooky at night on this little road, because the road bordered the river bottom land where bobcats, coyotes, and no telling what else lived in those woods. Some people thought there were panthers living there.

After we had driven approximately two miles along this road, there was a pipeline that crossed it, a line that ran for many miles across North Louisiana, owned by Texas Gas Company. The Texas Line was a favorite of the deer hunters who had their favorite locations along the line during deer season, areas where most deer being chased by deer dogs would cross the line as they raced toward the Ouachita River, where they would lose the dogs as they swam across the river.

To our surprise, on this night we found a car parked just off the road, on the pipeline, and we stopped to see who it might be. There was Van Gathright's car and he and his girlfriend, Barbara Jo Ward were sitting in the car, and Larry Scarborough was standing by Van's open car door, with a pistol in his hand.

Billy Tom cut his engine and left his car in the road. We got out of the car and walked over to Van's car as Billy Tom asked Larry, "What's going on here?"

"Aww, we're just sitting here in the moonlight, talking and killing time," said Larry.

"What's the pistol for?" I asked. "You think a rabbit may come by?"

"No," said Larry. "I'm going to play Russian roulette." He held the long barreled 22 revolver out to give us a closer look.

"Russian roulette? Have you lost your mind?" Billy Tom asked, as he laughed nervously.

"You've never played Russian roulette?" Larry asked.

"No, I have not! And I don't plan on playing it anytime soon either!" Billy Tom replied.

"Aww, you're just chicken," said Larry. "This is a nine shot pistol, so you have eight chances out of nine that it won't fire when you pull the trigger."

"That's crazy……not very good odds!" I said. "You're not really gonna do that, are you?"

With that, Larry laughed that little funny laugh, and then he pulled the hammer back on the pistol until it was cocked. He slowly raised the pistol up, pointing it at his right temple, and before we had a chance to say anything, he pulled the trigger, and we heard the snap of the hammer closing on an empty chamber. We were all shocked that he had actually done it.

The four of us watching this, almost in unison, told Larry that he was crazy, and he needed to put the gun away before he killed himself.

Larry only laughed at us. "Hey, I don't have anything to live for, so it wouldn't matter if I blow my brains out!"

It was confirmation to me that when Larry was drinking, he was more despondent and heartbroken over losing Justin Cooper. I knew it already, but until that night, after seeing him taking a chance of killing himself, I had not realized just how bad his heartbreak was. I pleaded with Larry, "Please, don't do that again!"

"Come on, you try it," said Larry to me as he held the gun out as if to hand it to me. "I know you got more guts than Billy Tom!"

"Oh no!" I said. "That is just crazy, for someone to do that! Come on, Larry, put the gun away!"

Larry only smiled at me, pulled the hammer back on the pistol and held the barrel up against his temple again, and this time he hesitated for a few seconds as he held the gun there. He pulled the trigger, and we all gasped at the sound of the hammer snapping shut. The sound of the pistol hammer as it shut seemed to be extremely loud to me as it interrupted the silence of the surrounding woods.

I challenged Larry after he chuckled at us. "Hey, you don't have a bullet in the gun, because if you did, you wouldn't be playing this stupid game!" With that, Larry reached in front of the cylinder that held the cartridges, pulled the release pin forward, and flipped the cylinder out. He pointed at the back of the cylinder and asked, "What does that look like?"

The moonlight shining on the gun revealed one cartridge in the cylinder, and as Larry quickly flipped the pistol to the right, the cylinder swung back into place and I heard the snap of the pin as it locked the cylinder in place. I was really scared now that I knew for sure there was a cartridge in the pistol, and instantly, the four of us began to beg Larry to quit playing his game, but he looked around at each one of us, slowly turning his face toward us, and with a faint smile, he stated once again, "I told y'all that I don't have anything to live for, so I really have nothing to lose!"

I'm sure the others were as afraid as I was that this night. We were going to witness the death of our friend, and I really thought it was about to happen in the next moment, as Larry once again cocked the hammer on the pistol and held it up to his head. "If this is the one, it's been good knowing y'all," he said with a solemn tone in his voice, and he then pulled the trigger as all of us yelled for him to quit this crazy game.

We made so much noise as he pulled the trigger that we did not hear the sound of the hammer striking the empty cylinder, but I could see as he slowly lowered the gun to his side, that the hammer had closed and his life had been spared once again. We were making so much noise trying to get Larry to stop it, we could barely hear him laughing at us. I couldn't believe he thought it was funny. I was scared so badly that I was almost sick to my stomach, and it made me mad that Larry thought it was funny. "Just what in the hell is so funny?" I yelled at him.

He continued laughing loudly, and he released the cylinder on the pistol and flipped it open again before reaching into his shirt pocket for his cigarette lighter. He flipped the top back on the Zippo lighter and with the spinning of the striker with his thumb, the lighter flared up. He held the lighter over the open cylinder and asked, "Do you see that little mark on the back of that cartridge?"

I had bent over and my head was within a foot of the pistol to see what he was talking about, and when I saw the mark he was pointing to, I realized that he had only an empty cartridge that had been fired previously in the gun. All along, he had been playing a huge joke on us, or it was what he called a joke. It was no laughing matter, because I had been convinced that Larry was going to blow his brains out while we watched it happen.

"You butthole, you ought to be shot, for scaring us so bad," I yelled at him, and the others agreed with me. After we got over our fright, we began to laugh at ourselves for being so gullible to believe that Larry would play Russian roulette with a live round in the pistol.

As a peace offering, Larry offered Billy Tom and me cold beers he retrieved from a small water cooler where he kept his beer on ice, sitting on the back floorboard of Van's car. We each took a can of beer from him, and he reached into the pocket of his jeans, pulled out a beer opener and handed it to Billy Tom, who punched two holes in the top of his beer and he handed the beer to me. "Here, you drink mine, and if you'll let me have yours, I'll drink it!" He laughed as I took the open beer and handed him the other.

I took a sip of the beer while Billy Tom was opening the other, and I told him, "I do believe that this one is probably the better of the two! I'm glad you swapped with me." We all laughed at the silliness of our comments about two beers of the same brand, out of the same water cooler of chopped ice. We needed that silliness after being so tense and frightened by Larry's antics a few minutes earlier.

Billy Tom and I left shortly after that and rode down to the Alabama Landing, where we saw Haney Lee Fisher, who worked and lived there in a two story shack of a house. Haney came out with a flashlight, with his little dog, Frisky, following along at his heels. Haney shined the light into Billy Tom's car as he reached the bottom of the stairs that came down from the living quarters of the shack, and after recognizing us, he walked over to the car and spoke to us. We only talked a few minutes, and we apologized to Haney for getting him up this late at night.

"That's alright. I had to get up to see who was here because there have been a few drunks that showed up here from time to time, and they want to give me a little trouble."

"I hate to hear that," said Billy Tom. "We'll see you later."

Haney had a slight speech impediment, and as he turned back toward the stairs, he spoke to his dog. "Come on Fwisky," he said to Frisky, which was unnecessary, because Frisky always stayed at Haney's heels wherever he went.

As we drove away from the Alabama Landing toward the Four Mile Post, we discussed the events we witnessed when we encountered Larry and his friends earlier. We chalked up Larry's actions to his sad state of mind, as he always seemed to be, in one way or another, mourning over his lost love. We felt his sorrow, but there was little we could do about it.

CHAPTER 10

Early Winter, 1961

EARLY WINTER BROUGHT out the hunters, and they hunted from the four mile post crossroads to the Alabama Landing on the river, and in the river bottom both north and south of the Alabama Landing. This area consisted of several thousand acres of hunting for squirrels, deer, quail, ducks and rabbits. This was where most of the hunters who lived around Haile and Linville came to do their hunting, and folks from a large area of north-central Louisiana duck hunted in the lakes and sloughs in the river bottom, mostly north of the Alabama Landing, and up to the Arkansas State Line where the Ouachita River entered Union Parish, Louisiana.

I could walk a half mile in any direction from our house and get in on a deer hunt during deer season. The McKinnie brothers, Joe Ollie, T-Boy, and Sugarboy always had good deer dogs, and also there were others that had dogs that they kept in good running shape by running foxes at night during the spring and summer, and then they ran deer during deer season. And then there was Sid Patrick, who ran a service station in Marion, and later was elected Town Marshall there. He may have a hound or two, but when deer season began, he would go to the dog pound in Monroe and pick up a half-dozen or more of mixed breed dogs they had there, and he would bring them and throw them out of the truck wherever a group of us wanted to get a hunt going. There would be poodle mixed, hound mixed, mongrels, and once he brought an Airedale that turned out to be a good deer dog. Some of the dogs wouldn't hunt and they would just wander off and would eventually be taken in by some of the folks who lived in the area. Others would chase rabbits or squirrels, and never get in on a deer race……Sid never knew what to expect from his menagerie, but it was always a source of entertainment for us deer hunters.

Edward Plummer, whose nickname was "Chop Chop", usually had two or three hounds, and he would get up a deer race on his own, or sometimes put his dogs out with the dogs of his uncles, the McKinnie brothers. After the first chase in the morning, there would be some of the pack of deer dogs that would chase the deer into the river, and most dogs would quit the chase there. But there would be some dogs that would swim the river after the deer, and their owner would either have to take a boat and cross the river in the evening, and blow their dog horns to try to call their dogs back to them. For those of you who don't know what a dog horn is, it is a cow horn with a short piece of the tip cut off, then an inch or so of that end was reversed and re-attached to the horn with glue. The reversed tip was drilled through, and when you blew through the tip with almost closed lips, it would make the sound of a loud horn, and no two horns ever sounded exactly alike. A man's dogs would recognize the sound of his horn after being called with it a few times, and his dogs would only return to the sound of this horn. If this did not work, the dog may eventually show up along one of the roads leading toward the owner's home, or return home in a day or two. At times, the dog's owner would have to go to Bastrop and up the 'Long Lonesome' they called it. This was a graveled road that stretched for miles and miles through woods north of Bastrop, along the river bottom where it tied in with the hills that ended in the lowlands called the river bottom. The dogs all had collars with brass name tags on them, listing the owner's name, address and telephone number, and many times someone in Morehouse Parish would hold the dog and call the owner to let him know where to come to pick up his dog.

I recall a rather humorous incident that happened one morning on the Charlie Lee Road near the point where it connected with the Alabama Landing Road. There were several of us hunters gathered at a pipeline crossing, and most of the dogs were scattered after the first hunt that morning. Sugarboy walked up to three others there and said, "Why don't we round up some dogs and try to jump another deer? Chop Chop told me a while ago that he saw old Traveler and Bawler cross the road down by the Interstate pipeline, and I heard Belle down toward Finch Lake about fifteen minutes ago, and probably old Speckles is with her. I could go back down the road and probably call them out to the road."

Goober Johnstone was standing nearby and had not spoken since he first arrived and said howdy to everyone after getting out of his truck five minutes earlier. Goober spoke up after Sugarboy's comments about wanting to round up dogs for another hunt. "I got old Red in the truck," Goober said in a slow drawl.

But no-one acknowledged that they had heard his comment. They just kept talking about what had transpired on the first hunt. There had been a doe that passed by a couple of hunters as Sugarboy's dogs chased it. Deer were not very plentiful then as they are now, because there were poor people who struggled to get by, and they would shoot deer illegally year round in order to have meat to eat. This included shooting does, and each doe killed meant that there would be one or two less babies born the following spring, and this caused the deer population to decline over a long period of time. Doe deer could not be legally killed at all during that time, according to state wildlife rules and regulations.

After a couple more minutes of small talk, Sugarboy said, "I'm know we can round up enough dogs to jump another deer."

After Sugarboy's comment, Goober again said in that slow drawl, "I got old Red in the truck."

And again, the others acted as if they did not hear what Goober had said. I was feeling bad for him because they appeared to be deaf to his comments.

Then there was more talk about various other subjects for several minutes, which was always what transpired when several hunters gathered together on a road or pipeline. It was part of the tradition of deer hunting, because many of these men seldom got together, unless it was deer season, therefore, they all had stories to tell.

One more time, I heard Goober tell them when there was a break in the conversation, "I got old Red in the truck." And again, he was ignored.

Finally, Sugarboy looked around the group, and he spoke to his brother, Billy McKinnie. "Billy, you go down on the Landing road and see if Traveler and Bawler have come back out to the road, and catch them for me. Chop Chop is down that way and he's probably got a couple of his dogs with him, and I'll go down toward Finch Lake and try to call Belle up, and Goober's got old Red in the truck, so we can get up another race."

Whew, I thought. I'm sure glad that he finally quit ignoring Goober. I know Goober thought nobody had heard him after telling them three times that he had old Red in the truck, while no-one acknowledged that he had spoken!

Goober was one of my favorite people. I always thought he seemed sad, but that was probably just me, because I had been told that when Goober was a teenager, he was driving a flatbed truck one day with several of his friends riding on the back, sitting along the sides of the flat bed. I don't know exactly what happened, but I think the truck crossed a hole in the road, or some type of rough spot that caused one of his friends to fall from the bed of the truck. The truck was going pretty slow, but his friend was thrown forward when he fell off the truck, and the rear wheel ran over him, and he died instantly. The person who told me about this tragic accident said that when Goober saw what had happened, he ran away crying and screaming in shock. This happened a long time before I first met Goober, but even before I was told about the accident, I sensed a sadness in him, but he seemed to be so humble and just one of the sweetest men I ever met. I was out of state on a construction project when Goober, who was retired from the oil field, found out he was terminally ill, and he took his own life. My first thought when I heard of his death, was that the loss of his boyhood friend that had haunted him the rest of his life, had ended, and surely they were reunited in Heaven.

A few weeks later, in late December, during the period when school was out during the Christmas Holidays, a couple of inches of snow fell on Union Parish, and snow in Louisiana always excites everyone, because it does not happen very often.

Deer season would be ending in the first week of January, so hunters were out in hopes of getting at least one deer before the season ended, and the snow brought with it the anticipation that the deer would be moving a lot more. I was up early, and bundled up with the warmest clothes I could come up with, and struck out walking toward the river. I had walked only about a quarter mile when Chop Chop pulled up beside me in his father's 1953 four door Plymouth, and offered me a ride. Larry Scarborough was with him and as I crawled into the back seat of the car, I heard some bumping noises in the trunk of the car, and I asked Chop Chop if he had some dogs back there.

"Yeah, I got two deer dogs back there," he said. "When I hear them bumping around back there, I know they're still alright. I had a sad deal day before yesterday. I was riding around looking for somebody to put on stands so I could have a deer race with my three dogs, but there wasn't anybody out. The dogs had been in the turtle hull for two or three hours and when I finally went home and opened it up to let the dogs out, old Lucy was dead as a hammer! I guess that leaking muffler and them rusted out holes in the bottom of the turtle hull caused Lucy to be carbon monoxided to death! Boy, I liked to have cried. Lucy was my best deer dog!"

"Oh man, I hate to hear that," I said. "You think them two dogs back there are O.K.?"

"Yeah, as long as I hear that bumping, I know they are O.K., because they don't like one another and they are always fighting a little bit when they're closed up together like that. But I stop about every thirty minutes or so since I lost Lucy, and I raise the turtle hull and let them get some fresh air, and let them exhaust fumes get out of there."

"That's good," I said. "I'd hate to see you lose another dog."

Larry looked over at Chop Chop and said, "You ought to let them dogs ride in the back seat, and then you wouldn't have to worry about killing them."

"Shoot no! I don't want to ride with them stinking dogs. I mean, I love my hounds, but I don't love to smell wet dogs after they been crossing creeks and such!" Chop Chop slowed down as he came to the Texas line where it crossed the river road they were on, and as he turned left to go toward the river, he pressed the accelerator to the floorboard and the old Plymouth spun the rear tires in the snow for about twenty feet before the tires quit spinning. The automatic transmission, in combination with the weak, six cylinder engine, would not generate enough torque to spin the tires unless you were driving on a muddy road, or in this day's snowy condition.

Larry looked back at me and held up a bottle of Seagram's Seven whiskey. "You want a shot of whiskey?"

"Yeah, I'll take a slug," I said, not really wanting it, but I didn't want them thinking I was a wimp. I took the bottle from Larry over the seat back and un-capped it. I took a small drink from the bottle, and before I put the cap back on the bottle, Chop Chop held his hand out toward me over the seat back.

"Don't cap it off!" he said. "Give me a shot of that whiz!"

With that, I put the bottle in his hand as I said, "Here, Larry, take this cap. Thank y'all for the drink."

Chop Chop kept trying to make the car spin the wheels as he drove down the pipeline toward the river. It was so funny because the old car was so weak that it would spin on the wet snow for just a wee bit and then it would quit, because it had so little power, it just couldn't do better.

Larry laughed at the sad effort the old car made, and he looked at Chop Chop, saying, "You better be glad that it will go, because that is what it's supposed to do. Your Daddy didn't buy this car to spin, he bought it to drive. He's not going to get in a rush as long as he gets to where he is going. That's all he wants." He didn't want to see the old car break down because of abuse. "Just keep it between the ditches. Hey, why don't we go up to see Dude Patrick? You know where she lives?"

"Yeah, I think I know where it is. Loco, ain't it?"

"That's right, I been there once before," said Larry. "I took Joe Eddie home one time last year. Boy, it is about as far as you can go in Loco, because a little ways past their house, there's nothing but gravel pits and then the swamp."

I was looking forward to the trip because I had never been past Lonnie Turner's house, and I thought the Patrick place was somewhere just beyond Lonnie's. I had been to Mr. Turners a few years before, when I was about eight or nine years old, with my daddy. We went to see if Mr. Turner had some pigs for sale.

Lonnie had built their house himself, and he used whatever he could find to build it. He built it with the ceilings just high enough that he could walk through it himself, but his wife was taller than he was, so she had to bend over when she walked through the house, and each of his boys were taller than he was before they got grown, and they had to bend slightly when they stood up after they were in their teens. This constant bending over caused Lonnie's wife and a couple of his sons to walk in a slightly bent over position as time passed. The house had dirt floors, so it had been really interesting to me. It was built on a hillside, and a section was added later as the family grew larger, and Lonnie built it on the downhill side, so it was lower than the original house. It was the first two story house that I had seen, but it really was not a two story, it was just a few feet lower in the newer section. I told my buddies at school how interesting the house was after I first saw it. It was built by a man who used whatever he could tear down when someone gave it to him and he just built one room when he got married and he added to it as needed, so it served its purpose. Many people were poor in the 1930's and on into the 1950's and they got by the best they could.

We headed up to Loco with Chop Chop driving, after he stopped the car and opened the trunk for a few minutes to let his dogs get a breath of fresh air. He wanted to make sure they didn't stay closed up so long that they would be victims as Lucy was.

Chop Chop was driving slow as he drove back down the pipeline toward the Alabama Landing Road, but he picked up his speed after he reached the road and turned right. A little less than a mile up the road, he turned right on the road that would take us through Dean and up to Loco. Larry and Chop Chop opened the bottle of whiskey a couple of times on the way to Mr. Patrick's, and took a sip from the bottle, then offered it to me, but I thanked them as I declined their offers. The straight whiskey was too much for me, but they were like most guys that drank whiskey, when it got cold, they drank it straight from the bottle, with no chaser. They said it made them warmer…..not me, it almost made me sick.

As we passed the Turner house, I wished we could stop and see the house, but Chop Chop only slowed down as he went by, so he could see the house that he had heard so much about. "Boy, I wish we could stop and go through that house," he said. "I'll bet it is really something to see, inside."

Larry and I agreed with Chop Chop, and I turned in the seat and looked it over as we drove on past it. When it disappeared from sight, I turned back toward the other two, and as we crossed a little bridge with no sides on it, I told them, "Pat Patrick's house ought to be just a little ways from here."

"Yeah, there it is right yonder, on the right," said Larry as he pointed at it. "I hope we get to see Dude."

I was surprised at Larry's comment, but Dude was a nice looking girl that I had seen a few times at church at Dean. She was a little older than I was, and I didn't know about whether she was allowed to date or not. She went to Marion High School and I figured she probably had a boyfriend anyway, so I figured Larry was wasting his tiime.

As we pulled up near the front of the Patrick's house, I could see that the front porch was pretty high above the ground, because the front of the house was on a slope that began just beyond the enclosed portion of the house, and it caused the porch to look odd in relation to the house. And out of the house came three or four boys, but no Dude, and that disappointed

Chop Chop and Larry, and they mumbled slowly before the car came to a complete stop. "Where's Dude?" said Larry.

"I don't know, but I hope she comes out here," said Chop Chop, as he stopped near the porch and switched off the engine.

Joe Eddie, the oldest of the boys, was leading the pack as they came out onto the porch. Cecil and Jimmy followed, and the little one, Jesse James, who was about five or six years old, followed them out. They all came down off the porch and gathered up together near the driver's door. When Joe Eddie saw Chop Chop, he knew him from when he went to Linville High School, before their home fell into the Marion school area after re-districting was done.

"Hey, Edward," Joe Eddie said. He knew Chop Chop only by his name he used in school. "How are y'all doing?" he asked.

"Doing fine," said Chop Chop. "This is Larry Scarborough," as he pointed at Larry, "and back there is Freddy Ray Franklin," he said as he held his arm up, sticking his thumb back toward the back seat. "You know them, don't you?"

"Yeah, I do," he said. "How y'all doing'?" Joe Eddie asked as he leaned over, looking into the car.

"We're cold," said Larry. "I saw the smoke pouring out of that chimney, as we was pulling in here. I bet y'all got a big fire going in that fireplace."

"Yeah, this little snow is nice, but the weather is too cold since it snowed," said Joe Eddie. "It's too cold to stay outside very long."

He looked down the road and saw a little boy who appeared to be about the same age as Jesse. He was Jack Allen Turner, and he was walking up the road toward them. "Hey Jesse, I see Jack Allen this side of that culvert. You better run him back over to the other side of it. You know he ain't supposed to be on this side of it!"

Joe Eddie's little brother, Jesse cursed Jack Allen as he took off running to the road. I heard him yelling at Jack. "You better get back on the other side of that culvert, you little bastard," he yelled, as he bent over in the middle of the road and began scratching in the snow, picking up rocks as he reached them under the snow.

Down the road, I watched as Jack Allen Turner ran back down the road until he reached the culvert, and as soon as he got beyond the culvert, he began scratching snow off the roadway, and he was picking up rocks. He picked up as many as he could before Jesse got closer, and then he ran a little bit further away, and he turned back toward Jesse and he began throwing the rocks he had picked up. Jesse dodged as he continued to run and he began throwing at Jack Allen.

They were busy throwing rocks and yelling at one another until they ran out of rocks, and then they began scratching in the snow on the road trying to get more ammunition, but the rocks were harder to find down near the culvert, so Jack Allen ran toward his house so that he was out of range of the few rocks that Jesse found. He yelled something at Jesse and he ran toward the house in the distance. Jesse stood there a minute watching him run, and then he turned and began walking back toward us.

"Boy, they don't like one another, do they?" Chop Chop said to Joe Eddie.

"No," said Joe Eddie. "If Jesse sees Jack Allen cross over on this side of that culvert down there, the fight is on. But Jack Allen usually runs back home, because he knows that Jesse will tear his little butt up if he catches him."

All the boys laughed at that, but the fight was serious to these two little boys. The Patrick brothers were sure that sometime in the future, the two would forget whatever the fight was about, and they would become good friends again. But for now, the feud was ongoing, and it was good entertainment for the older boys.

And Jesse James Patrick and Jack Allen Turner would become good friends a short time after this incident, and after they were grown men they continued to be good friends until Jack Allen drowned while swimming in the Ouachita River at the Hooker Hole. Jack Allen had not reached the age of thirty when he drowned, and Jesse James drowned due to a boating accident on the Ouachita River, just north of the Alabama Landing, before he reached the age of forty. Jesse was going fishing and soon after heading up the river, the wind lifted his coat up from where it lay on the boat seat in front of him, and while attempting to catch it, he temporarily released his grip from steering the motor, which caused the boat to suddenly turn, and he fell out of his boat and drowned in the cold river.

Larry and Chop Chop continued visiting with Joe Eddie for a few minutes, and for some unknown reason, neither of them asked about Dude. They stated their intentions to return to the hunt near the Alabama Landing, and after saying their goodbyes, Chop Chop cranked the car and pulled out onto the snow covered road and headed back to where they came from.

"Dang it," said Larry. "I wanted to see Dude! Why do they call her Dude? Her name is Eloise."

Chop Chop shook his head from side to side before speaking. "I don't really know, but I think Joe Eddie told me one time that their Daddy, Pat Patrick, started calling her Dude because she would always wear his cowboy hat whenever he would pull it off, back when she was a little girl. Pat would call her 'Dude' because she acted like she thought she was a little dude, and the nickname just stuck with her brothers."

"Oh, I see," said Larry. "Hey, give me a shot of that whiskey. I'm thirsty." He pulled on Chop Chop's heavy coat lying on the seat between them, and after finding the bottle of whiskey there, unscrewed the cap on it and took a short swig of the whiskey before passing it on to Chop

Chop, who took a drink and stuck the bottle back under the coat after he capped it off.

I declined when Chop Chop asked if I wanted a drink from the bottle. I thought to myself that Larry did not really want to see Dude, or he would have asked Joe Eddie if he would bring her out of the house while we were there. I knew that Larry somehow always had Justin on his mind, and he really did not want to have another girl get in the way of this, but he needed something, and I was not sure what that was. And I didn't think Larry even knew himself what he needed to do at that time.

CHAPTER 11

※

Winter, 1961 & 1962

WINTER SLOWED US down and we did not see each other as much as we normally would, because it was tough to walk or hitchhike to Haile due to extremely cold weather, and especially hard to subject myself to possibly having to walk the five miles back home in the middle of the night on the weekends, in such conditions. But there were times when I would ignore the possible hardships I would face by going out to Haile on Saturday afternoon, and I would hit the road walking, hitchhiking, not knowing what would be in store for me at midnight, when the other boys would head home.

Basketball season at school was going on and I was a starter on the team, but my junior year of school was the worst for me because I made it hard for myself, with my smoking and drinking, and I was at my worst for doing things that no other sensible teenager would do. I don't know why I acted as I did, but It appeared that I would never do as I was expected or as I was told to do at school. My hair was extremely long for 1961, and I was a punk who existed in a system that seemed foreign to me. The things that my classmates enjoyed did not interest me, and I acted as if I were hell bent on ruining my chances of completing my school year.

Basketball was still in the early part of the season and it ended for me after I floored a player who elbowed me in my face early in the game, and I did not get my chance to get him until there was less than two minutes left in the game. When the referee's whistle blew, I walked off the court to the dressing room and dressed out. Earlier, during the game, I had also shown some disrespect for an opposing coach who was scouting our team while he sat on the stage above our bench. I was out of control and I got what I deserved the following morning when I got to school.

Early that next morning someone informed me that I needed to see Coach Till in his office in the gym. When I walked into his office, he first asked me why I walked off the court and dressed out before the game was over the night before.

"Well, it was only a minute and thirty seconds left in the game, and I heard you tell Joe to take my place, so I didn't figure I would be put back in the game after I busted that guy's butt."

"Well, that was no reason for you to just walk away from the game! And why did you intentionally knock him down?" Coach Till asked, and this was the first time I had seen him really mad.

I told him that the guy had one coming, because he had elbowed me across my face in the first part of the game.

"I want to know something else. Why did you say what you did to Coach Jones?" Coach Till asked, and I could tell he was furious.

"Well, he kept ragging me, and I just got enough of it!" I replied. I was mad myself now, even though I knew that I had been so disrespectful and wrong.

"I have had it with you, and I want your uniform!" Coach Till yelled at me. "You will never play ball for me again!"

"That's fine!" I said, and I walked out, down the stairs to my dressing room locker, and took the basketball uniform out of it. I took the uniform back up to Coach Till and gave it to him, then walked out.

I met my older brother, Gerald, who was a senior, and he had his basketball uniform in his hand, heading to the Coach's office. When I asked him what he was going to do, he told me he was quitting the team.

"Man, don't quit because of me!" I told him. "I needed to be kicked off of the team, but you don't need to quit!"

"Awh, I've just had enough of this," Gerald replied. "I don't want to play basketball anymore."

I knew that Gerald must have heard Coach Till express his intentions of kicking me off the team, on the night before, and he was quitting because of what he had heard. I felt bad that this was happening, but it was not enough to wake me up to my failures in school that were mounting up as time moved on.

On some basketball game nights at Linville after that, I would show up, many times after drinking beer with the older boys, and I was almost always out of control. Don Jenny had shown me how to blow a ball of fire from my mouth, using cigarette lighter fluid and a Zippo cigarette lighter, and I never saw Don do that but the one time when he showed me how it was done. But I would do it sometimes in the gym, and over time, I would squirt more and more lighter fluid into my mouth, and I would blow larger fire balls as time went on. I became more isolated from the students in my class during that winter and I became closer with the older boys who were more like me, defying actions that seemed normal to others.

As 1961 ended and January of 1962 came, the news from Baton Rouge continued to bring grief to Larry Scarborough, as it brought news to him that Justin was soon to have a child. No one at Linville really knew what was going on in Justin's life, and I don't know exactly where Larry got his news about her, but I knew that he was still checking on her regularly. I did not know how many of our friends knew how much Justin's absence and the apparent loss of her affections for good was affecting Larry, but I talked about it with Billy Tom Ellis when we were out together, and I, for one, was deeply concerned about it, because it was affecting Larry greatly.

Larry spent much of his time in his 1956 Oldsmobile, riding around Haile and Linville, listening to the radio, and he had his favorites, usually really getting into the sad songs. Some of his favorites were *Crying*, by Roy Orbison, *Sea of Heartbreak* by Don Gibson, *Stand by Me* by Ben E. King, and *The Duke of Earl* by Gene Chandler.

Many times during the winter of 1961/1962, I rode with Larry and others as we listened to the radio and just shot the breeze about whatever crossed our minds, and that would cover a lot of ground. We talked about so many things, just enjoying the conversation and the company of friends who happened to be in the mix at the time.

During most of these times, Justin Cooper's name was never mentioned, but we all knew that she was on Larry's mind every day. If you were around Larry, there would be a time when he would seem to be oblivious to whatever was going on around him. It may be only a few seconds, or it may last a moment, but you would know he was somewhere else for that moment. We could only assume what these brief moments meant.

We knew Larry was getting some information, very little it seemed, but he received some information as to what was happening with Justin in Baton Rouge. On February 26, 1962, Justin gave birth to her first child, Kelley Hinton. And though Larry did not mention it to me, I think he knew about the birth soon after Kelley was born, but he didn't know that Justin and her husband, Charles Hinton, were already separated and would never get back together.

CHAPTER 12

Spring, 1962

SPRING OF 1962 brought with it baseball, and I had been through the worst of the most rebellious year of my life, and after being kicked off the basketball team the previous fall, I was beginning to make a turn for the better. Coach Billy Till was, first and foremost, a really good person, and he had dealt with me as he should have at the time. The events that occurred the night he made the decision to cut me from the team were all mine and the result was, I think, the turning point in my life that began to steer me back in the right direction. But there was yet to be many bad decisions that would be made by me, but I think this was to be the beginning of a long and arduous battle to get to where I should be and where I wanted to be.

Coach Till began to quiz me long before baseball season began about my desires and my plans for the future, and he had asked me if I thought I could mind him and do my best to rid my life of the demons that ruled me. He would never know the real reason for what I carried with me during this time, for he died of a heart attack while he was still a relatively young man. No one outside my family would know until many years later that I had tried to kill my father, while protecting my mother, when I was only nine years old.

Coach Till agreed to give me a second chance, upon the conditions that I would do my best and I would listen to him and do as he asked me to. If I would promise him to do so, he would allow me to play baseball that spring, and if I kept my end of the bargain, I could play basketball and baseball during my senior year. I promised him I would do my very best.

But there would still be that rebel inside of me that ruled my life outside of school, and I continued to drink on the weekends, and smoke every day, therefore, I never reached my full potential in sports, and I only applied myself just enough to make passing grades in most of my school classes. And I continued to run with the older guys, some of them grown men, decent, hardworking people, each who had their own personal and individual problems or situations that ruled their lives. We were bound together, though, with the same sense of helplessness that pointed us toward lives of oilfield roughnecks, or mechanics, or some type of labor to provide a future for us and eventually, our families.

The weekends would find us in groups of three or four in someone's car, running together, making a trip to the Arkansas state line to buy beer, riding around the countryside, going to the river, or anywhere else that kept us on the move, talking about anything, whether we knew about the subject or not.

It seemed to me that we concentrated on the music most of the time. We listened to a couple of stations that we could only pick up at night. One of those stations was supposedly in Del Rio, Texas, and the other was Randy's Record Mart in Gallatin, Tennessee. We also tuned into the local stations that played a mixture of country, rock and roll, or rhythm and blues.

There were so many great songs and singers during that time, and you could hear someone like Acker Bilk, performing the beautiful instrumental, *Stranger on The Shore,* the Shirelles with *Soldier Boy,* Gene Chandler with the *Duke of Earl,* the great Sam Cooke, Nat King Cole, Connie Francis, The Everly Brothers, Booker T and The MG's, and the list goes on and on, with songs that covered so much territory that I would listen to the radio every chance I got, in order to hear the good music. The radio was basically a teenager's main source of entertainment out in the country during that time, and we heard songs that were popular during the late forties, all during the fifties, and the current songs. All of them would be in the mix as the radio stations played songs that covered so much time and types of music. The late fifties and the early sixties changed music probably more in a few short years than at any time in the history of the music industry. There were just so many great singers, such as Don Gipson, with *Sea of Heartbreak*, Peter, Paul & Mary, who sang *If I Had a Hammer*, the Beach Boys, Paul Anka, Brenda Lee, Roy Orbison, Elvis, Jerry Lee Lewis, and there were so many one hit wonders who had great songs, and then they faded away. It was such a fantastic time for someone who loved all types of music, and I was one who definitely loved it. And my friend Larry Scarborough, shared my love of music, and he reacted to it in a very personal way, for the heartbreak he was going through, and the music spoke to him.

The spring of 1962 brought with it a release by Ray Charles, an album called *Modern Sounds in Country & Western Music*, a record that showed the greatness of the singer. It was an album of country music that featured some of the best songs ever written in that genre, and two of the songs included on that album were *Born To Lose,* and *I Can't Stop Loving You*, and these songs would quickly become Larry Scarborough's favorite songs of all time. When I was riding with Larry and one of these songs came on the radio, I quickly learned to say nothing, and I listened and I could feel his pain and heartbreak as the song, whichever it might be, played. Larry would quickly reach for the volume knob on his radio and turn the volume up so the music would take over, and those of us riding with him would know that he wanted to hear nothing but the song!

Franklin

It has been said many times that Ray Charles was a genius, and though he ushered in Rock & Roll with *What I Say*, which changed everything, and his musical tastes covered such a broad spectrum, I think the "genius" title bestowed upon him definitely fit when he created *Modern Sounds in Country & Western Music*. The use of an orchestra with the many beautiful violin arrangements, plus his talented backup singers, especially in the song *I Can't Stop Loving You*, was breathtaking, and I understood Larry's instant attachment to that song, especially as I was witnessing, from week to week, month to month, the toll that the loss of his sweetheart, Justin Cooper, was taking on him. And there was nothing I could do, or so I thought. In my mind all I could do was sympathize with Larry. I know there were others who felt the same way, but for some reason, the heartbreak I was witnessing during that time has stayed with me since then, as a lifetime of caring and wishing there had been some way I could have helped Larry.

But I just rode with Larry, and I was silent when his two songs played on the radio during that spring.

Though it has been many, many years since that time in my life, and I have been blessed with a family that continues to increase, and the duties and responsibilities have increased greatly for me during all this time, *Born To Lose* and *I Can't Stop Loving You*, by Ray Charles, always takes me back to that time and they make me as sad now when I hear them played, just as sad as they did then.

It was during that spring when Larry's strong attachment to the song *Born To Lose* caused a great deal of concern for me, as I realized how much he was suffering with the loss of his love. In some way, I felt the song was prophetic, and I searched for signs that Larry might be feeling that his life was going to end in some tragic way, but I knew this was unlikely, for he was a young man who had so much going for him, and I felt that he would get beyond this and move on with his life.

96

There were times during that spring when friends would be riding around with Larry, and there would be a mix that would be different almost every time, but many times I would be along because I was one who didn't have his own car, or I didn't have the use of my dad's car. It seemed that always, at some point during our rides, the songs by Ray Charles would come on the radio, and there was always that gap in the conversation as the radio was turned up by Larry, and conversation would resume when the song was over and Larry turned the volume down. I don't really know how much the others were aware of the real meaning of these interruptions, because we seldom talked about it, but I do know that some were aware of Larry's fascination with the songs and they also knew his reasons for that fascination. But I was certainly aware that there was this heartbreak silently chewing away on Larry's heart, and for the most part, it seemed that most of the other friends in this circle did not take the matter as seriously as I did. But I did know that with each one, their friendship with Larry was every bit as strong as mine was, and I would venture to say, there was probably a couple that had a stronger bond with him, simply because they had been friends with Larry for a longer period of time.

I have had a number of dark times in my life, some that were evident in my life as a child, the seventh son who longed for what was coming next, knowing somehow that I was to see things that others did not see, and feel things as no other would feel them. But it still makes me wonder, to this day, why I have always felt that the spring of 1962 was a time which was marked with a feeling that I was witnessing something that would stay with me the rest of my life. As I look back on that period, it seems that I was such a loner, I had no close friends in school, only those I ran with on the weekends, and my classmates and even my own family did not understand whatever it was that made me act the way I did.

I continued to walk, or hitch hike, the five miles to Haile each Saturday afternoon, to meet up with those few friends who I felt comfortable with, Billy Tom Ellis, Sidney Ray, Don Jenny, Billy Hill, Edward "Chop Chop" Plummer, and Larry Scarborough. There would be others who spent time with us, and many nights we would build a fire out from Ed Thomas' store, and we would stand around the fire talking and drinking beer until the fire burned out. As the fire slowly died, the group would get smaller as those with vehicles of their own would slowly drift away, leaving the few who would always seem to run together to close out the night. Many times, there would be one who would offer me a ride home, and at other times, the last couple of boys who had vehicles there would bemoan the fact that they were almost out of gas, and they would apologize to me as they drove away. When I wound up being the last one there, I would sit on the bread box under the front of Thomas' Grocery and wait for Parker Haile to come from his girlfriend's. If he took the backroad behind the stores to his house, that would signal to me that Parker did not have enough gasoline in his car to drive me home, and I would begin the five mile walk to my home, and this would take an hour and a half, whether it was on a full moon or on a pitch dark night. I knew the road so well, that the only difference would be, on the dark nights, I would watch the treetops alongside the road where the three bridges I had to cross were located on that stretch of road. As I came to those bridges, I would drift over to the middle of the road and slow down as I watched the treetops for the very moment I would be crossing these short bridges, because they did not have any railings on the sides of the bridges, and I was afraid I might walk off the edge of a bridge if I did not exercise the utmost caution when crossing them. It always worked, as I never even came close to the edge of any of the bridges, even on those nights when I could hold my hand eight inches in front of my face, and I could not see my hand. I had plenty of time to think about what had transpired during the night, and to try and forecast what may come as time moved forward, and I always envisioned a brighter future for me and my friends. I always felt fortunate when I caught a ride home, but I was never really bothered when I had to walk that five miles, because I was fully aware that more than likely, I would be on my own and walking in the end. I could not help myself, because my desire to get out of the woods was so strong that I was not bothered by the thought of walking that distance after midnight.

On most nights during this spring, while I made these five mile walks, I would sing to myself the three songs that Larry Scarborough loved so, *Born To Lose* and *I Can't Stop Loving You*, and *Sea of Heartbreak*.

The first verse of *Born To Lose*:

Born to lose, I've lived my life in vain
Every dream has only brought me pain
All my life I've always been so blue
Born to lose and now I'm losing you

The second verse of I Can't Stop Loving You:

Those happy hours that we once knew
Though long ago they still make me blue
They say that time heals a broken heart
But time has stood still since we've been apart

The chorus of Sea of Heartbreak:

The sea of heartbreak
Lost love and loneliness
Memories of your caress

So divine, how I wish
You were mine again, my dear
I'm on this sea of tears
The sea of heartbreak

It had occurred to me that two of the three songs had been recorded by Don Gibson, a wonderful country songwriter and singer, and they would be the songs that Larry Scarborough would listen to as many times as he could. *Sea of Heartbreak,* written by Paul Hampton and Hal David, was a hit for Don Gibson in 1961, and he had a hit with *I Can't Stop Loving You,* which he wrote, and he recorded it December 30, 1957 and released in 1958. The two songs that Ray Charles released in the spring of 1962, *Born To Lose,* written during the 1940's by Ted Daffan, and *I Can't Stop Loving You,* were both hits for Charles, but the latter was huge, and can still be heard on the radio today, and these three songs touched Larry in a special way, and in turn have always been very special to me.

The spring of 1962 has always been a special memory for me, and in a large part, the music makes it special, but the joy of being sixteen years of age, and being with friends who shared my sense of freedom, not thinking very far ahead into the future, made it a time that can only be felt as a teenager. Most of my rowdy friends would face their future soon, but I had one more year left in high school, which meant that I would enjoy that much more time before life met me head on.

CHAPTER 13

Baton Rouge, June, 1962

MAY BROUGHT WITH it the end of the school year, and my brother Gerald would graduate at the top of his class, and with scholarships, which meant he had a real chance to go to college and would not have to face the prospect of trying to figure out what type of labor he wanted to do for the rest of his life. He, along with my friends Billy Tom Ellis, Don Jenny, Armond Love, and others in the graduating class of 1962 were subjected to making the decisions that may possibly determine what direction their lives would take from that point forward.

Earlier in the year, Larry had sold his 1956 Oldsmobile after he saw a 1957 Ford for sale, a two door hardtop that was black with red trim and an Interceptor engine under the hood. He fell in love with the car and he loved the response he got while driving it when he pressed his foot down on the accelerator. In addition to the looks of the car, he loved the acceleration and the speed. With the help of his father, Clint, he was able to buy the car.

I was slightly adrift, knowing that all of my running mates would be heading off in different directions soon and I wondered what I would do. There was little time to dwell on it, but for the next few weeks, with us being free for the summer, we ran the same routes we had been taking for a long time, and I enjoyed it while I could.

I never knew where Larry was getting his information about Justin Cooper, but I knew his source was limited in their knowledge about her. This I know because it was at some point in May when he heard that she may be divorced from the man she had married less than a year ago, and he quickly devised a plan to follow up on this news and possibly re-connect with his lost love. Larry didn't tell me about the rumor, but he told me he was going to look for work in Baton Rouge, and he asked if I wanted to go down there with him to look for work.

"No," I told Larry. "I'm not eighteen years old yet, so I doubt that I could get a job making decent money, and if I did, I would have to quit at the end of August, to come home and start my senior year at Linville High."

"Man, I wish you would go with us. I think Billy George and Billy Tom are both going with me, and I wish you would."

"I appreciate that. I really would like to go, but I would hate to get down there and not be able to go to work because of my age," I told him. And that was the end of our discussion about Baton Rouge. I felt so honored that Larry had asked me to go with him, and I also felt bad about having to turn his invitation down.

He was right about Billy George McKinnie and Billy Tom Ellis in that they wanted to go to Baton Rouge, because there was not much going on in the gas field around Haile, and the few rigs that were drilling gas wells in the area had crews that had been with them for a while, so there was little chance of getting a job as a roughneck. The three of them decided to make their plans and drive to Baton Rouge as soon as possible.

Larry had made the decision to strike out to Baton Rouge on Monday, June 11, 1962, and Billy George and Billy Tom agreed with him that the sooner they got there, the sooner they could expect to be hired. Larry had recently quit his job with Allen Brothers Hatchery, the first thing he had to do in preparation for going to Baton Rouge.

Early on that Monday morning, Larry left home in his 1957 Ford, first picking up Billy George at his home three miles from Linville before driving back to Ed Thomas' Grocery in Haile, where Billy Tom was waiting for them. Billy Tom was to drive his car to Ferriday, Louisiana, and leave it with his brother, Harvey Ray Ellis. Larry and Billy George would pick him up in Ferriday and he would ride on to Baton Rouge with them.

They agreed that Larry would follow Billy Tom and they headed out for Ferriday, and from there on to Baton Rouge, and each of them was looking forward to being hired for who knows what. But Larry had more to look forward to than either of the other two boys, because he was hoping to see his long lost love, Justin Cooper, and he was sure that they would take up where they left off, and his life was about to get a lot better. He shared little of his thoughts with his friends, but he was excited at the possibilities that this trip brought with it.

The three arrived in Baton Rouge well before noon that day, and they immediately stopped at a convenience store and bought a newspaper to look through the want ads in order to make their plans to look for work. They decided to go to an employment agency that listed openings for a number of jobs that they considered themselves qualified for and also would suit them if they were successful in getting hired.

They went back into the store and purchased a Baton Rouge city map, and after looking up the address of the employment agency, they discovered that it was located relatively close to the northern portion of the city where they had stopped to begin their search. They decided to get something for lunch before heading out to the agency.

After a lunch of hamburgers at a drive in, the three studied the map and drove to the address and after unintentionally passing by the employment agency, they turned around, drove back to the agency, and parked in the parking lot of the building where the agency's office was located.

Upon entering the building, they met the receptionist, who directed them to the gentleman who would interview them in order to determine the type of work they were interested in. After his initial questions were answered, he learned that the positions in the agency's advertisement in the Baton Rouge newspaper were the ones they were interested in. The gentleman called the bread company that was featured in their ad and made arrangements with the personnel director to meet with the three young men at 9:00 a.m. the following morning. After filling out the forms that listed their personal information, each of them were given a form to sign that would authorize the agency to collect their fee from the bakery in the event the men were hired, plus a sheet of introduction to the personnel manager at the bread company. The meeting and the completion of the paperwork took less than thirty minutes, and after the gentleman explained to the boys that if they were hired, the employment agency would receive their payment from the bakery, and that money would be deducted from their first month's pay. They were informed that they would not be required to return to the employment agency unless they were not hired by the bakery, and in that case, they would be referred to other companies in search of employees.

After leaving the employment agency, Larry pulled into the first supermarket parking lot and parked, in order to check the newspaper ads for rooming houses or boarding houses in the northern part of Baton Rouge. They found several listings and agreed to check out a rooming house which they found to be in the northwest portion of Baton Rouge a few miles from the place where they hoped to go to work soon. Larry followed Billy George's instructions as he read the map while Larry drove to the rooming house, which they arrived at within fifteen minutes, and after looking it over, the price seemed to be a real bargain, so they signed in and were given a room with two beds, a refrigerator, and a private bathroom.

The first thing that Billy Tom did after they had checked in to the rooming house was, after double checking the address, he filled out a postcard to send to his girlfriend, Carolyn Nale, listing the address of the rooming house, and telling her he would call her after they found jobs and got settled in. He placed the card in the mailbox on the street corner at the end of the block.

After placing their few belongings in their room, Larry suggested to the other two that they ride around Baton Rouge and familiarize themselves with the city. They had been told that almost any kind of business could be located along Airline Highway, and after riding several miles down Airline, they realized that they could find just about anything they would want or need somewhere on this divided highway. They turned around and headed back up Airline Highway and turned toward the location of their rooming house as it was late afternoon, and they decided to get back there in plenty of time to go by the small grocery a few blocks down from where they would be staying to buy some bread, cold cuts, and whatever else they would need to make sandwiches.

When they returned to their room, the three of them made ham sandwiches, and then they left the room to sit in the lobby for a while after eating, where they searched through the many magazines in the racks adjacent to the couches and chairs, for whatever interested them, and that was mostly the magazines that featured cars.

CHAPTER 14

Failed Contact

LARRY WAS RESTLESS, and he thumbed through a magazine for a few minutes without really paying much attention to what he was seeing. Soon he placed the magazine back where he had found it, and turning to Billy George, he said, "I'm gonna walk down to that telephone booth on the corner and make a call. I'll be back in a little while."

"O.K.," replied Billy George, looking up briefly. "If we're not out here when you get back, we'll be in the room."

Larry walked through the door and down the short flight of stairs to the sidewalk that would lead out to the sidewalk beside the street, looking to the right to make sure that was where he remembered the phone booth was. It was there at the end of the block, on the opposite street corner, and as he walked to the corner and crossed the street after the traffic cleared, he spotted a young man in dirty work clothes in the booth, so he walked on by to the middle of the block and lit a cigarette. He stuck his Zippo lighter in the right front pocket of his jeans, and with the cigarette hanging from the corner of his lips, he pulled his wallet from his left rear pocket before getting the lighter completely back in his pocket.

He was nervous as he flipped his wallet open and reached for the small piece of paper on which he had written Justin's sister's telephone number. Larry had once met Grace Marie Cooper, but he almost felt as if he knew her well from the many times Justin had talked about her during the time he and Justin were dating over a year ago. The two sisters were very close, and Justin, along with her baby girl, Kelley, were living temporarily with Grace Marie. Justin was taking courses at a business school, and with Kelley being only four months old, there was little time for Justin to do anything but take care of the baby and do her studies at night.

When the young guy walked away from the telephone booth, Larry quickly walked back to the booth, and upon entering it, he placed the paper with Grace Marie's telephone number on the small shelf below the telephone, then he reached for the change in his left front pocket and laid it on the shelf beside the paper. He took a deep breath, removed the receiver from the phone, and placed a dime in the slot on the telephone, and dialed Grace Marie's number.

The phone rang several times before someone answered it, and there was a woman's voice on the other end. "Hello," she said.

"Hello," said Larry, "Is this Grace Marie?"

"No, she is here, but she can't come to the phone right now. Can I take a message for her?"

"No. Is Justin there?"

"Justin is not here, but I think she will be here in the morning, if you want to call back then."

Larry hesitated for a few seconds before replying. "Can you tell me if Justin is still married?"

"Who is this?" the young lady asked.

"This is someone from Haile, and I just wanted to know if Justin was still married."

The young lady then hesitated a few seconds before asking again, "What is your name?"

Again, Larry refused to answer the question, and he asked once more, "I just want to know if Justin is still married?"

The young lady did not know anything about Haile, and even though Justin had been separated from her husband, Charles Hinton, for quite some time, and was in the process of obtaining a divorce, Grace Marie's friend told Larry, because he refused to identify himself, "Yes, Justin is still married."

Upon hearing the answer he did not expect to hear, Larry slammed the telephone receiver back onto the hook without saying another word, and he stood there several minutes, with his head hanging down, his chin almost on his chest. No-one could ever know what was going through his mind during that time, but it must have been the most devastating news, because he had anticipated this moment for a long time, but with much different results. He had dreamed of re-connecting with Justin for a long time, and the news he had just received had completely floored him.

Billy Tom had walked a couple of blocks down the street to a service station to purchase a pack of cigarettes shortly after Larry had left the rooming house, and as he was returning, he saw Larry standing in the telephone booth across the street as he walked by. He wondered briefly about why Larry was standing in the booth with his head down, but he dismissed it without much thought, but later, the scene was replayed in his mind several times, and he knew the answer.

Larry slowly walked back to the rooming house, as the disappointment he suffered from his call to Grace Marie Cooper's house began to sink in. What would he do now? What could he do now? He felt as though he had very little hope of ever being able to re-connect with Justin, and he was literally devastated. He did not want to go to the job interview that was planned for the next morning, mainly because he now had no desire to be working and living in Baton Rouge, so close, yet so far away from the love of his life, who apparently was still married. This was contrary to the rumor he had heard in May, and he must have felt as if his whole world was crashing in on him.

Larry walked into the room after entering the boarding house, and he immediately begin to express all his frustration and disappointment he felt from the results of his phone call. He expressed his thoughts and feelings as he had never before to anyone about how much he cared for Justin Cooper, and he told his friends that he was finally convinced that there was no hope for the rekindling of his romance with Justin.

Billy George was very sympathetic towards his cousin who had been his close friend since early childhood. He had never, at this point in his life, been in love as deeply as Larry had been for such a long time now. He did not know what to say or do to comfort Larry in his misery, and for the first time in his life, he felt completely helpless. But he tried to give Larry some hope that there may be an opening somewhere in the future for him to see Justin, and maybe even start over with her,

"I know how much she cared for you," he told Larry. "You could tell she was crazy about you when y'all were together while she was at Linville!"

"Yeah, but that was a long time ago. Now she has been married for over a year and she has a little girl, and I doubt that she will ever leave her husband," stated Larry, as he stared at the floor.

"You don't know," said Billy George. "Anything could happen. You know yourself that she possibly could have had to get married, and if that's the case, there's a good chance that they may split up before long!"

Billy George's comments did not seem to have any effect on Larry, and he sat there not speaking for a long time. Eventually, he expressed his desire to go back home and try to go back to work at the hatchery.

Larry remained silent after he mentioned the hatchery, so his friends did not talk any more as they seemed to be really interested in the magazines they had been reading when Larry had entered the room. But they were both concerned as Larry lay on the bed next to the wall and stared at the ceiling, where he lay for another hour without saying a word. The bed Larry was on was at the opposite side of the room from the small table where Billy George and Billy Tom sat, and the floor lamp behind the table provided enough light for them to read, but the far side of the room where Larry's bed was did not receive much light from the lamp, so he was more or less isolated from the other two boys.

After all that time had passed, Billy George placed the magazine he had been reading on top of the two or three extra magazines on the table, and he stated his intentions of getting ready for bed as he walked into the bathroom. Billy Tom looked over at Larry briefly and then he stared down at the magazine on the table in front of him, but he wanted to talk with Larry about their plans for the next day. He decided to just wait until Larry said something, because he knew that Larry was not in the mood to talk at all.

A few minutes later, Billy George came from the bathroom and sat on the edge of the first bed, pulled his boots off, but left his socks on and he just laid back on the bed and doubled his pillow up under his head. He didn't say anything for a few minutes, but Larry finally looked over at Billy George and began a conversation.

"What do you think I ought to do?" he asked Billy George.

"Well, we got these interviews scheduled for 9:00 tomorrow morning, and I think you ought to go talk to these people," Billy George replied as he rolled over on his right side and looked at Larry.

"I don't want to talk to anybody, and I sure don't want to be working here close to where Justin and her family are living. Not if I can't see her!"

Billy George looked over at Billy Tom, who appeared to be immersed in the magazine, even though he was listening to the other two and only appeared to be disinterested. "Billy Tom, what do you think Larry should do? He's saying that he don't want to go for that interview in the morning."

"Well, we came down here looking for work," Billy Tom said as he looked up. "And I think we ought to give it a shot."

Larry returned his gaze to the ceiling above his bed for a minute or so before finally speaking. "I'll think about it, and I'll let y'all know in the morning what I'm gonna do."

"O.K.," said Billy George. "That's good enough." And he rolled back to his original position on the bed and doubled the pillow up under his head as the room got quiet again.

After the lights were turned off, Billy George and Billy Tom were soon asleep, and Larry lay in bed by himself, wide awake and thinking of Justin. He wished he could dismiss her from his mind, but no matter what he did, his thoughts would return to her and he would go back over the conversation with Grace Marie's friend earlier in the evening. Maybe he should have called back later and talked with Grace Marie......maybe the conversation would have revealed something to him that would have given him some hope. He just needed something to pull him up from the depression he was sinking into, yet the more he thought about it, the depression continued to build and it was overwhelming him. He decided that he could not stay in Baton Rouge. In fact, he could not stand the thought of even staying the rest of the night. He needed to get away, and he needed to do it now, not tomorrow, or the next day, but right now.....tonight!

He rolled over and sat up on the side of the bed, hesitating in the decision he had made. He didn't want to wake up Billy George and Billy

Tom, but he knew he had to awaken them. The choice for them would be to leave Baton Rouge with him, or they would be left here without a car if they stayed behind.

Larry stood up and walked slowly in the dim light around the end of the two beds, until he was beside the bed where Billy George slept, and as he leaned over and gently shook Billy George by his shoulder, he was surprised by how quickly his friend woke up.

"What is it?" asked Billy George.

"I'm gonna head back to Haile right now, and I need to know if y'all want to go with me."

"I don't know. I thought you were going to make up your mind in the morning," Billy George answered quietly.

"I've been thinking about it, and I just decided a few minutes ago, I need to head back right now. I don't want to spend the night in Baton Rouge. Now if you want to go with me, you had better gather up your belongings, and you better wake up Billy Tom and see what he wants to do!"

"Billy Tom......Billy Tom......wake up." Billy George saw that Billy Tom was awake as he rubbed the backs of his hands across his eyes. "Larry is leaving and heading back to Haile, and he's wanting to know if we want to go with him."

"I don't know. What are you gonna do?" Billy Tom asked.

"Heck, I don't know. I know I need to go to work, because I borrowed money from Daddy to come down here!"

"Well, if you stay, I'll stay with you, but if you decide to go back to Haile, I guess I'll go back too," Billy Tom replied as he was getting out of bed, and he walked over to the floor lamp and switched it on.

Billy George threw the covers back and he got up from the bed. "Larry, why don't you stay until the morning, and if you still want to leave, you can leave then. But I think I'm gonna stay because I need to make some money."

"Yeah," said Billy Tom as he looked at Larry. "Man, I wish you would stay, at least until the morning, like Billy George says!"

Larry had remained silent, but after Billy Tom spoke, he looked at him, and then at Billy George, and he spoke with authority. "I have made up my mind, and I am heading back to Haile right now, and y'all can go with me if you want, or you can stay here. I don't care, but I'm heading north!"

"Well, Larry, I'm staying, because like I told you, I need the money! And you know there ain't no work at home! You may be able to go back to work at the hatchery, but we don't have a choice!" Billy George had made up his mind. "But I sure wish you would stay here with us!"

"I'm staying here too, Larry," said Billy Tom. "I'm just about broke and I need to go to work. But I'm like Billy George.....I wish you would stay with us!"

"There's no use in y'all trying to change my mind! I am going back to Haile, and I am leaving just as soon as I can load up my stuff!" Larry turned and walked into the bathroom, where he picked up his shaving kit and stuck his toothbrush and toothpaste in it and brought the kit out into the bedroom and laid it on top of his suit case. He walked to the corner of the room close to the foot of his bed, where he reached for the bar under a shelf on the wall, and retrieved the hangers that held a couple pairs of his jeans and three or four shirts. While holding his jeans and shirts in his left hand, he leaned over and grabbed the shaving kit, placed it under his right arm, and then picked up his suitcase with his right hand.

As he walked toward the door that opened up into the hallway of the building, he had a grim expression on his face, and Billy Tom would tell me later, it seemed that Larry was in a hurry to leave because it seemed he was trying to fight back tears. "Y'all take care of yourselves. I hate to leave y'all here, but I don't blame you, because I know you need to go to work. But I have to go!"

"You be careful on that road," Billy George said as Larry made his way to the door.

"Yeah, Larry, take care. Man, I wish you would wait until morning. It's 11:30 at night, and that's mighty late to head home!"

"I'll be alright," Larry said as he sat his suitcase down to open the door. "I'll see y'all." He picked up his suitcase and placed it out in the hallway, shut the door, and he was gone.

Billy George and Billy Tom both stated their wishes for Larry to be alright, worried about his leaving so late, and talked about him being so sad with the news that Justin was still married. And they went back to bed, but it took both of them a long time before they were able to sleep. They were worried about Larry, and wondered how they would manage without transportation until they could get Billy Tom's car from Ferriday.

CHAPTER 15

June 11/12, 1962

LARRY LEFT THE rooming house and headed for Haile, Louisiana and home, a four hour drive, and once he got outside the city limits of Baton Rouge, beyond the street lights, the highway was dark, and there was little traffic on the road.

He was headed up Highway 71, and it was approximately eighty miles to Bunkie, the first town of any size on his journey, and there must have been so many thoughts running through his head about where his life would go from here. Larry knew it would be over an hour before he could reach Bunkie, and the long stretch of mostly straight highway would be an ideal drive to gather his thoughts and begin to make plans for his future without Justin Cooper being a part of his life. But somehow, he knew in his mind, she would always be there, and he could not stop loving her.

The day had been long, and eventful, and Larry was tired. After the couple of hours he had spent lying in bed thinking about Justin before leaving Baton Rouge, and almost another hour on the road with her on his mind, he had to be getting weary of searching for any signs of hope, and he surely must be getting sleepy, driving on this dark, lonely highway after midnight.

No one knows for sure what was going through Larry's mind after he left his friends in Baton Rouge, but with that which had transpired within the few hours before he headed home, you have to think that it was all heartbreak for him and his mind was completely occupied with where he would be if he had gotten a different report when he called Grace Marie's house.

It was getting close to 1:00 a.m. when the long day caught up with Larry, and as he was meeting an eighteen wheeler headed for New Orleans, he apparently fell asleep at the wheel, and he drifted over into the south-bound lane on the two lane highway, and just before meeting the truck head on, the truck driver swerved over into the northbound lane in order to avoid a head on collision. The moment that Larry's vehicle ran off the left side of the pavement, he awakened and jerked the steering wheel to bring his car back up on the roadway, and in that instant, the distance of ten feet would have resulted in a completely different outcome, but Larry's car did not travel the other ten feet, as it struck the enclosed trailer's wheels located near the rear end of the trailer, and Larry Scarborough died almost instantly in the collision, as his car was trapped under the side of the trailer and dragged a short distance before the driver could stop the truck.

There were so many different scenarios that, had any one of the many occurred, it would have changed the outcome of that tragic night. My first thought, when I heard about Larry's accident and his death, was that if I had accepted his request to go along on this trip, I don't think I would have let him leave Baton Rouge alone that night. I was sure that I would have left with him and I would have kept him from falling asleep, or I might possibly have been driving. But it is said that our days are numbered, and only God knows when our time comes to leave this world. That has been my comfort for all these years since that terrible night that affected Larry's family so deeply, and others who also loved Larry. He had so many friends who were deeply affected by the death of this friend, this close friend, this young man who left a deep impression on those that knew him in this community of Haile, Louisiana, and the surrounding area, where everybody knew almost every person for miles and miles, and Larry Scarborough had no enemies anywhere. I don't remember him ever saying anything bad about anyone, and this gentle nature had endeared him to many.

There is a neat story that Jerry Owens told me about when he and Larry were classmates in the fifth grade at Haile Elementary School. The school was a two room school, where one teacher taught the first, second and third grades in one room, and the other teacher, Mrs. Callie Reppond, who was also the school Principal, taught the fourth and fifth grades in the other room.

Boys will be boys, and one day the fourth and fifth grade boys decided to have a boxing tournament at school (without the knowledge of Mrs. Reppond). Someone had brought two pairs of boxing gloves to school, and the boys drew names for the matches. Jerry Owens drew Larry Scarborough's name, and he thought, "Oh Lord. Larry is bigger and stronger than I am. I have had it!"

Their fight would be the first, so they went around to the side of the school building, out of the view of the two teachers, and drew the outline of a boxing ring in the dirt. When Jerry and Larry stepped into the imaginary ring, they began to bob and weave as they had seen boxers on television do in their fights. They exchanged a few punches to the body, and then Jerry threw a punch that he said would not have knocked a lamp stand down because it was such a weak punch. But to Jerry's amazement, Larry went down like a rock, and he lay motionless on the ground.

There is no way that this could happen in a public school these days, with parents always concerned about their children's safety, and also fighting in school is definitely not encouraged or tolerated. But this was a different time and place; this event did take place, and it provided a memory that would be recalled with fondness for a long time.

Jerry was shocked at the turn of events because he knew there was no way he could have knocked Larry out. But there in the dirt lay his opponent, apparently out like a light. When this happened, four or five of the girls who had been watching the fight ran over to Larry, with one shouting, "Oh no. Larry! Larry!" One of the girls who rushed over dropped to her knees beside Larry and sat back on her heels. She picked Larry's head up and cradled it on her lap. The other girls gathered around them, expressing their concern for Larry as he lay there, seemingly unconscious. They were very emotional with their comments and the concerned expressions on their faces.

Jerry was confused by all of this, thinking that the champion was supposed to get all of the adulation. He always thought "To the victor goes the spoils", and to him, something was not right about this picture.

Jerry looked down again at Larry, knowing that there was no way he could be unconscious, and what did Larry do at this point? He opened his eyes slightly, grinned at Jerry and winked, then he closed his eyes.

Jerry realized at this instant that Larry was way ahead of him in knowing how to deal with the girls. Here was the kid who should have been the winner of the fight, laying there in the dirt with his head on the girls lap, and he was pretending to be knocked out. To Jerry it seemed that somehow, Larry knew exactly what he was doing. And it certainly seemed to be working well for him because he was receiving all this sympathy from the girls, while the champ was being completely ignored.

After all these years, Jerry Owens remembers the events of that day as though it happened yesterday.

It was before daylight when the resident Louisiana State Trooper of Union Parish knocked on Clint and Myrt Scarborough's door, and delivered the terrible news that all parents dread, and news that they never want to hear. And in this case, that was the dreadful news that their beloved son had died in an automobile accident. Their world would never be the same from that day forward. These parents, who I knew well, the parents who treated Larry as their equal, parents who were his friends, and he a friend of theirs, they were two of the best parents a young man could hope for, and they treated all of Larry's friends with so much respect and caring. I had been estranged, for the most part, from my father for a long time, although my mother was such a special, loving person, and I envied Larry's relationship with his parents.

Justin Cooper, who was attending a business school, stayed at Grace Marie's house that day because she had been told by Grace Marie that Larry was supposed to call her, but the call she received later that day was a call from Parker Haile, in Union Parish, and his call was made to deliver the news of Larry's death. She was devastated because she, like Larry, had been hoping for them to re-connect, and after finding out later that week from Billy George, that Larry had not gotten the correct information when he called the day he was in Baton Rouge, she was even more devastated.

Larry's friends, Billy George and Billy Tom, did not learn of Larry's death until Wednesday, even though he died on Monday night, for no-one knew how to contact them in Baton Rouge. Billy Tom's girlfriend, Carolyn Nale, received the postcard from him Wednesday morning in her parents' mailbox, and he had given Carolyn the address of the rooming house where he and Billy George were staying, and had written her a note on the card that he would call her later in the week. Carolyn and many others were so worried that the two friends would not be located in time to come home and attend Larry's funeral, and Carolyn was greatly relieved to get that postcard with their address listed on it. She immediately notified the Union Parish Sheriffs' Office of the address, and that information was relayed to the Louisiana State Police, who sent a Trooper in Baton Rouge to deliver the news of Larry's death to the boys. Billy Tom would tell me later that when the State Trooper knocked on their door at the rooming house in Baton Rouge, and upon opening the door, he knew immediately that the Trooper was bringing bad news.

The two young men were horrified upon receiving the news of their friend's death, and after informing the Trooper that they did not have a car, he assured them that he would get them to the bus station.

Billy George and Billy Tom quickly gathered up their belongings that morning and checked out of the rooming house. They walked hurriedly to the State Police car, and the Trooper loaded their belongings in the trunk of the car and took them to the Continental Trailways bus station in Baton Rouge. After the Trooper dropped them off at the bus station, Billy George bought bus tickets to Ferriday, Louisiana for himself and for Billy Tom, and from Ferriday they would complete their journey home in Billy Tom's car. Neither of them remembered years later Billy Tom's reason for leaving his car at his brother's home in Ferriday when they were on their way to Baton Rouge.

At Larry's funeral later that week, there was an overflow crowd at Liberty Baptist Church, and he was buried in the Liberty Cemetery beside the church. It was such a sad event, as most funerals are, but a teenager's funeral brings with it so much sadness because a young person has their life ahead of them, a life beyond their childhood years, and it seems that a life cut short at that point is truly tragic.

Justin Cooper attended Larry's funeral and later, she and her four month old daughter spent some time with Larry's family at their home in Haile. She was so saddened by the death of this young man she had been in love with, and she explained to Larry's parents that she did not want to leave Linville High the year before, but said that she really had no control over the matter. She was sent back to her grandmother in Baton Rouge, and she had made the mistake of marrying Charles Hinton, and she had left him seven months later, at the end of 1961, and she was pregnant. The divorce would be completed soon, and she had wanted to talk with Larry after she found that he was in Baton Rouge. It had been so terrible that Larry had been unable to talk with her or at least with Grace Marie on the night he had called. Justin realized there had been a huge misunderstanding when Larry talked with Grace Marie's friend, and deep down, she felt that this breakdown in communications was responsible for Larry's death.

Justin and Kelley stayed with the Scarborough family for almost a week after Larry's services and the time spent there was special for Justin, and it was good for Larry's parents and his younger brother, Doyle. She got to spend very little time with Betty, Larry's older sister, who had married Benny Baker several years before. They had children, and even though they only lived about ten miles away, they were so busy that they were unable to spend as much time as Betty would have liked while Justin was there.

I spent some time with a number of Larry's friends over the next couple of weeks, and was told of the damages to Larry's car, from those who had seen pictures of the car after it was hauled to a wrecking yard in Bunkie. Billy George McKinnie was one of the guys who had gone down to Bunkie to pick up Larry's personal belongings, and he brought back with him Larry's aluminum safety cap he had found in the trunk of the car. The cap was commonly referred to as a "hard hat", and Larry had purchased it earlier that year because it would have been a required safety item had he gone to work on a drilling rig. The bright, shiny aluminum safety cap had never been used. Billy George showed the safety cap to me, and the rolled rim that encircled the cap, including the bill of the cap, had a dent in the rim that had to have been the result of an extreme blow to the rim. The dent was about an inch wide and it had crushed the rim of the cap inwards almost an inch near the back of the cap. It amazed me that there were no other dents at all on the cap, because I could not imagine there not being some damage to the opposite side of the cap from the dent. It would seem to me that the dent would have been made by something metal, and surely the cap was trapped between whatever it was that struck it and some other item or part of the interior of the trunk itself. No-one would ever understand or solve the puzzle of how the single dent had been made to the hard hat.

There was much sorrow among Larry's friends afterwards, and his name always came up in our conversations when we were together on the weekends, and there was a change in our attitudes about our driving habits because of what had happened with Larry. I had my driver's license, but I seldom had a chance to drive because my father would not let me drive his old truck until after I started my senior year at Linville that fall, and it was almost impossible for me to get his permission to drive the truck.

But the guys I caught rides with did drive a little slower, and they were more careful, and more conscious of the road conditions, and of everything concerning their driving. This made me feel a lot better when I was in their cars with them, for there had been times in the past when I had been afraid to ride with some of them, because it is no secret that teenage drivers can be reckless and subject to take too many chances while driving.

As time passed, the boys who had graduated from Linville in May, began to drift away from the Haile area, moving to jobs or to look for work. A few were drafted into the Army, and a few joined the other services to avoid the draft, and a few started college. The ones that stayed around Haile only stayed a few months, so my circle of friends became smaller as time went on. My friends I went to school with all had more sense than I did, and their parents monitored their activities a lot closer than mine did, so I didn't see much of them during the summer.

By the time school began at the end of August, I heard Larry's name mentioned less and less, and I thought how sad it was that so many of his friends seemed to be moving on with their lives, and were leaving Larry's memory behind. I still thought of him every day, but little did I know at the time, there were others who felt the same as I did, and over time, I would find that I was not the only friend of Larry's who felt this sorrow.

Years after Larry's death, Don Jenny's younger brother, Tommy Joe, told me about a whiskey bottle that Don kept with him for the rest of his life. It was a Seagram's VO bottle that he and Larry had shared a couple of weeks before Larry died. The two of them had been riding in the country-side on that day, sharing their thoughts and dreams as they were preparing to move forward with their lives as adults. I seldom saw Larry drink any-thing but beer, but the fact is that Don's bottle was a reminder of his last day with his good friend, Larry Scarborough. And as I had carried Larry's memory with me from that time in our lives, Don would use that bottle as a reminder of how special his last day with Larry had been, not for the whiskey, but for the friendship shared.

Billy George and Billy Tom, the two friends who had spent the last day of Larry's life with him, remember his final words to them as though it was only a short time ago, along with all the events of that day. And those memories are theirs for life, and I have shared with them a number of times, my memories of Larry, and there are others who spent time with him who will keep his memory alive, at least until our days are over here on earth.

CHAPTER 16

September, 1962

I WAS BACK in school and was bored with it, but I was glad that I was in my senior year, and that did make things better. I made up my mind to do better in school this year because I was growing up, but it would take me about fifteen years to complete that process. I always told my friends that I was a clear cut case of arrested development, in jest, but it actually was the truth, or at least in my mind, it was true.

Billy Tom Ellis had been living in Ferriday with his brother, Harvey Ray, but shortly after school started, he came home for a few weeks to try and figure out where he would go to look for work. He had a brother living in Dallas, Texas, and he was thinking that Dallas may be the place for him. I did not try to discourage him, because even though he and I were a lot alike, cousins and friends, I knew he would sooner or later have to leave home to make a start somewhere. And I knew I would miss him whenever he left.

Billy Tom and I had been through some pretty crazy days over the past couple of years. When I was fifteen, we took an axle from a wagon that his father abandoned and we made a crude buggy that we pulled with Dollie, their little red mule. We made one trip to Haile with this contraption and on the trip back home, it began to rain and Billy Tom used a switch to urge Dollie into a gallop, but he made the mistake of sticking Dollie's rear end with the switch. Dollie kicked both back feet up as soon as the switch touched her, and in that full gallop, her back feet came up on each side of Billy Tom's head and her right back hoof struck me lightly on my shoulder. Billy Tom thought it was really funny, but I told him in no uncertain terms, to never do that again. We survived that trip and the buggy was retired after that.

There was always something going on in our younger days to keep us entertained, and Billy Tom was a master of improvisation. He once took a hood that came from a thirties model car, turned it upside down, and rigged chains to the front of it so he could pull it with Dollie. The pointed front and the curved sides of the old car hood made a perfect ground slide that Billy Tom used to make trips into the river bottom land behind their home. Most people in the fifties and early sixties that owned a small farm would have a slide with a frame made from 2" x 10" and 2" x 4" lumber, with a floor made of 1" x 6" boards. You could ride in the slide, or walk beside it while a horse or mule pulled it, sliding it along the ground, to haul vegetables, potatoes, or watermelons, etc. from the fields to the storage sheds.

It was on a Saturday night while Billy Tom was home in September when he came to pick me up to ride around and talk before he left the next week to go to Dallas to stay with his brother, and to look for a job.

We rode down the highway from Haile to Sterlington, where we stopped into the Dairy Queen to get hamburgers and to listen to the jukebox. Our good friend, Don Jenny, who had graduated in May with Billy Tom, came into the restaurant while we were there, and he was talking of marriage soon. He and Charlotte Peterson had been dating for most of their high school years and it was always assumed by Don's friends that they would be married after high school. Not a lot of high school graduates went on to college after high school during that time, because a guy usually began to look for a job as soon as he received that high school diploma, and as soon as he could afford to marry, he would do so.

Don Jenny was a good looking young man who had blonde hair, and he had a great personality. He was a closer friend to Billy Tom than even I was, and the fact that they were in the same grade in school probably made that difference. But the three of us were good friends all through high school and beyond. During the previous school year, after I had been kicked off the basketball team, I ran with Don more than I had in the past. I reminded Don of the night he taught me to blow fire from my mouth, and we had a good laugh about some of the times I had done that after that night.

After Don visited with Billy Tom and me for a while, he had to leave, so we left the Dairy Queen and headed back toward Haile, listening to the radio, with Billy Tom driving slower than usual. It seemed as if he was trying to slow time down and I felt that he was really dreading the thought of leaving home for Texas. The radio station we were listening to played *Stand By Me* by Ben E. King as we rode through Spencer, and it seemed to get his mind off leaving. Later on, the station played *Cryin'* by Roy Orbison, one of my favorite singers, and we talked very little as we just eased along the highway, with no particular place to go. Billy Tom turned off the highway at Haile, and drove by the Haile Baptist Church, and he continued down the road all the way to the Hooker Hole on the Ouachita River. He pulled down close to the sand bar on the river's edge and cut the engine off and we sat there talking for probably over an hour. We talked about some of the crazy times we had in the past, and as we looked out at the river at the water glistening in the moonlight, I thought about a near tragedy that occurred back in the summer that involved Larry Scarborough's younger brother, Doyle.

I realized that Billy Tom was not aware of this, as he had been with his brother and his family in Ferriday, Louisiana, since shortly after Larry's death. "Let me tell you what happened a while back," I said. "We almost lost Doyle Scarborough while we were swimming right here! He came so close to drowning when he swam across the river with us, and he either suffered from cramps or he got too tired to go on while swimming back from the other side of the river! What a terrible tragedy that would have been, if the family had lost both of their sons in such a short period of time!"

Billy Tom agreed that the loss of their other son would have been such a tremendous tragedy for the Scarborough family. "Tell me what happened," he said.

I rolled my window down, pulled a cigarette from the pack of Winston's in my shirt pocket, and after lighting the cigarette, I began to tell Billy Tom the events of the day that began as a group of teenage boys having fun swimming in the river, and ended with near fatal results.

I told Billy Tom that I had been with a group of friends swimming here in the river one Saturday afternoon when some of us decided to swim across the river. In addition to me, there was Tommy Crain, Paul Meeks, Doyle Scarborough, and a couple of the others in the group as the ones who chose to swim across to the other side and back. There were several other teenage boys there who chose not to attempt this marathon, but Doyle decided to go with us because he had swam across the river and back several times before in the past. Even though he had not planned to swim when he came to the river that day, Doyle removed his shirt, boots and socks, and he was ready to swim with only his blue jeans on.

The river at the Hooker Hole was approximately one hundred and twenty yards from shore to shore, so it was not an easy task to swim that distance non-stop, but for teenagers who were athletes, it was fairly common for some of them to make that swim. Doyle was a strong young guy, one who did not participate in sports as much as the rest of us, but his decision to swim the river did not concern any of us at all. We swam across the river in a group that stayed pretty close together, and as we climbed out of the water on the far side, there was not much sand along the edge of the river there, and the growth of brush began just beyond the sand, so we stood in a line along the water's edge to rest before swimming back to the other side.

There was not much conversation as we stood there, but we all agreed that swimming the river was about as far as any of us wanted to swim non-stop, and the few minutes of rest was definitely needed before swimming back to the other side.

We had not been there long when Doyle Scarborough waded into the water, which deepened a short distance from the edge, and as the water got up above his waist, he began to swim alone out into the river. The rest of our group stood watching Doyle as he swam, but no-one seemed to be quite ready to go back into the water at the time.

All at once, Doyle, not halfway across the river yet, stopped swimming and began to splash about in the water with his hands. We did not realize that he was in trouble until he sank underneath the water, and as his head came up out of the water, he yelled, "I can't make it! I'm not gonna make it!"

Paul Meeks immediately dived into the river and began to swim toward Doyle, but the four of us left standing at the water's edge did not immediately respond. For a moment, I thought Doyle was pranking us and he was really just taking a break from swimming, and I don't know, but I assume the others thought the same. But before Paul got close enough to Doyle to help him, he went under the water's surface once more, and he came up spitting water out of his mouth, and he yelled again, "I can't make it!"

At that point, we knew Doyle was not kidding, and we almost panicked as each of us jumped into the river and began swimming as fast as we could toward Paul and Doyle. Paul reached Doyle shortly after he surfaced and there was a struggle for a couple of minutes, or it seemed to me to last that long. As Doyle, in his fright, continued to yell that he was not going to make it, and he was clinging to Paul, which caused both of them to sink momentarily beneath the water's surface, I really began to get concerned. But my concern soon changed to pure fright, because Paul was fighting to get Doyle to release his grip on him, and he was yelling loudly at Doyle, telling him that he was going to cause both of them to drown if he did not let him help instead of clinging to him.

Paul's yelling did not seem to sink in with Doyle, so Paul jerked away to loosen Doyle's hold on him and he shoved him toward the far side of the river for a couple of feet, but as he did, Paul sank beneath the surface. As Paul surfaced, he swam a couple of strokes and then he shoved Doyle again, moving him forward maybe three feet, and he continued to do so as Doyle calmed down some and the yelling between the two stopped.

At this point, we had not caught up with Paul and Doyle, and as we got nearer to them, Paul seemed to have a plan that was working pretty well, but he was tiring quickly. I, for one, did not realize the toll it was taking on Paul to keep Doyle moving toward the shallow water jutting out from the sandbar at the far edge of the river. All of us were a bit weary after swimming across the river and then swimming rapidly half way back toward the other side. I was swimming along maybe ten to fifteen feet behind Paul and Doyle, and I assumed that since Paul appeared to have the situation under control, he did not need any help.

Paul continued to struggle until he was within a hundred feet of the shore, and he yelled at the group of swimmers in the river's edge to come out and help him, and at that point, a couple of them swam out to meet them, and with their help, Doyle actually attempted to swim some as they guided him to the shallow water that extended approximately thirty feet out from the river bank.

I felt so terrible afterwards, as Paul, exhausted from his heroic efforts in saving Doyle from dying in the river, explained to me that he was completely exhausted after fighting Doyle and pushing him toward safety, and he told me that God gave him the strength to continue pushing Doyle ahead. Paul told me almost every time he pushed Doyle that he himself would sink into the water and his head would go under, and this made it hard for him to get enough air to keep going. I wondered why I did not have enough awareness to see just how much Paul had been struggling, and why neither me nor any of the other three did nothing but watch as our friend struggled through this ordeal.

After I finished telling Billy Tom about this near disaster, he sympathized with me about our lack of action that day. "You know, sometimes you just don't realize that you are witnessing something that is that close to turning into a tragedy, and you can't blame yourself for not seeing this at the time. Thank God that everything turned out as it did!"

"Thank you," I replied, and we sat there in silence for the next few moments.

With God's intervention that day, Doyle's life was spared, and I witnessed a hero in action, saving the life of a friend, and since that time, I have realized that outside of combat during wars, there are very few of us who get to see something as special as someone saving another's life.

And I never swam across the Ouachita River after that day!

Eventually the conversation between Billy Tom and I got around to some of the good times we had with Larry Scarborough, and we talked of how much we missed him.

"Larry's funeral had to be one of the saddest days in my life," Billy Tom told me, and his voice had a sadness in it that I had never heard before. He stared out at the middle of the river, where the water glimmered from the moonlight that provided just enough light for us to be able to see the opposite side of the river, where the water appeared to be black.

"It was sad for me, but somehow, I guess I was still in shock, because I didn't cry at Larry's funeral. I haven't cried since my old man kicked me in my ribs while he was climbing across me in his old truck when he made me drive because he was drunk and I got the truck stuck in the middle of the road. I wasn't even eight years old and I couldn't drive, but he made me drive until all the slack in the steering wheel caused me to lose control and get stuck in the middle of the muddy road. He didn't really mean to kick me, but it hurt like hell, and I cried. And I swore I would never cry again!"

"He made you drive? How could you see over the steering wheel?

"Well, I didn't. I looked through the top of the steering wheel, and I had to sit on the edge of the seat to do that! Once I got to moving, I thought it was funny, but after I fought that slack in the steering wheel of that old truck until I got crossways in the road and got stuck, it wasn't funny after that! The old man was mean when he was drunk!"

"It don't sound like he was too bright," Billy Tom laughed as he said it, but then he got serious again. "You know, I didn't cry at Larry's funeral either, and I don't know why. I have never lost someone close to me before, not in my family or a friend, and that funeral really got to me, but I didn't cry."

"I couldn't really believe he was gone," I said. "Maybe that was why I didn't cry, but during that funeral, I did think about what I told myself that day in that old truck, that I would never let anything make me cry again!"

I asked Billy Tom to tell me about the night that Larry died in the car wreck. I wanted to know what he said to Billy George and him before he left them that night, and I wanted to know again why they couldn't talk Larry into waiting until the next morning to leave Baton Rouge. Billy Tom went back over the story that I had already heard a couple of times before, and though I didn't say anything to Billy Tom, I wished once again that I had accepted Larry's request that last time I saw him, when he asked me to go to Baton Rouge with them.

After that, as we were silent for a while as we watched the movement of the river, I asked Billy Tom if it would be o.k. for me to switch the car radio station, as the station it was on was fading in and out as the local stations always did at night. He agreed that anything would be better than the station of mostly static. I tuned in to XERF-AM, whose disc jockeys proclaimed that it was the most powerful radio station in the country. Well, it was not actually in the country. Although it seemed to be coming to us from Del Rio, Texas, the broadcasting was actually done in Ciudad Acuna, Coahuila, Mexico, because it was licensed for 250,000 watts, and stations within the United States could only be licensed for 50,000 watts. The DJ would play rowdy rock and roll music, along with raw rhythm and blues, and they would have commercials that featured some crazy items, and in addition to that, the radio personalities were different from any you would hear anywhere else. This was one of the couple of radio stations that we could only receive their signal at night. In that year, a new voice came on the air at XERF, and he called himself Wolfman Jack, and he would howl and keep you entertained between songs and commercials. One of his favorite sayings was "If you got the curves, baby, I've got the angles," and the first time

I heard him say that, I had to think about it for a bit before I got the meaning of it.

After we sat listening to the radio for a while, Billy Tom reached for the key, cranked his car and switched on the headlights before he spoke. "Well, you know and I know how much we cared for Larry, and that's all that counts." He drove up from the river bank to the dirt road that would take us back to Haile, and again he drove slowly as we made our way out of the woods in the river bottom.

Billy Tom decided after listening to XERF for a while, he had grown tired of the station, and he switched the radio to Randy's Record Mart on WLAC in Tennessee as we reached the highway at Haile and he continued driving toward Linville. WLAC was a 50,000 watt clear-channel station in Gallatin, Tennessee, and this was the other station we could tune in only at night. We would listen to Rhythm and Blues records that we were more familiar with, usually played by a host who called himself John R., and we heard music that was not available on any of the local radio stations.

At the midway point between Haile and Linville, Billy Tom turned left on the side road that would take us by the cemetery at Liberty. We had talked very little since we left the Hooker Hole, with Billy Tom driving slowly as we listened to the radio. I had a feeling that Billy Tom was headed for the cemetery, but I did not know what to expect when we got there.

A gas well had been drilled at the end of the Liberty Cemetery, and there was a dirt drive that provided the gas company meter reader access to the well to change the chart monthly. Billy Tom turned into the drive and stopped his car at the gas well location, where he turned off the ignition and the headlights. We both got out of the car and walked over to the cemetery fence which was just low enough that we could step over the fence by standing on our tiptoes and pushing down with our hands on the top of the fence.

There was enough moonlight for us to see as we worked our way around tombstones until we arrived at Larry Scarborough's grave site, which still had a couple of wire stands on each side with plastic flower arrangements on them. As we walked up close to the grave, Billy Tom picked up the flower stand on the right and moved it further away from Larry's grave, and I did the same with the stand nearer the grave marker. Neither of us had spoken since we had driven past the church on the hill above the cemetery.

We both got down on our knees by Larry's grave, and we sat on our heels as we silently stared down at our friend's grave. After a couple of minutes, the silence was broken by the hushed crying of both of us as we seemed to come to terms with the fact that the reality of the situation was that our good and close friend was gone, and our emotions had taken over. We cried for several minutes there, and that was a moment that was frozen in time for me, and I'm sure Billy Tom felt the same way, for it seemed a weight was lifted from me, and we had honored our friend with our tears, which is the way it should have been.

I don't really know how long we stayed at the grave site, but we finally stood up and returned the wreath stands to their original positions, and we turned and walked away slowly, stepped back over the fence, and returned to the car. We drove away from the cemetery, and after several miles, Billy Tom spoke for the first time since our conversation ceased as we drove past the church at the cemetery.

"I feel so much better now that I have had my cry over Larry," he said. "It has really been bothering me since Larry's death that I could not find any tears for him!"

"You know, I feel the same way. I had begun to feel like I was cold hearted, as much as I thought of Larry, I just could not find a way to cry for him until tonight. I really appreciate you taking me to the cemetery, because being that close to Larry tonight, made me realize how much he meant to me and how much I'm going to miss him!"

"Yeah, we needed that. And I'm gonna be leaving here in a few days and I don't know when I'll be back, so I can take that with me, where ever I go!"

As Billy Tom pulled up by the front gate at my home, before I opened the door to get out, I thanked him again for everything that he had done for me the last few years, and especially for this night.

"You be careful, and I'll see you before you leave for Texas," I said before I shut the car door.

"You bet. I'll see you. Goodnight," he said. And he pulled back onto the road and drove away.

CHAPTER 17

Winter 1962/1963

As Autumn changed to Winter, I was occupied with trying to make passing grades, and playing basketball, and as I had played very little basketball since the season ended in my Sophomore year, I was a bit rusty, but I would get better as the season progressed, and I was much more settled than I had ever been in school. I had been voted as a favorite in a category or two in the the yearbook elections, and that was such an honor for me, as I had always been so critical of myself. I was elected president of the Future Farmers of America, and was also co-captain of the basketball team along with Johnnie McKinney. My senior year of high school was shaping up to be the best school year I would ever have, with a total of sixteen students who graduated in the spring of 1963.

Due to me being at the height of my rebellious youth the previous year, I had actually failed the eleventh grade, but with the help of Mrs. Norma Hobgood, our English teacher, I was given the opportunity to make up for that in order to graduate with my classmates. Mrs. Hobgood was sort of a rebel in her own right, and she butted heads with our Principal, Mr. Alton Hollis, at times, and also with some of the other teachers, but she won my admiration by standing up for me to help me graduate. I was someone who had shown little prospects of ever being successful, with my attitude as a rebel, and a poor student, yet Mrs. Hobgood saw something there that I think no-one else saw in me, including myself. It took me some time for that to sink in with me, but once it did, I tried to prove myself a worthy candidate for the faith that she placed in me. You might say that rebels will stick together to survive, or it seemed that way to me. I don't think Mrs. Hobgood ever really knew how much I loved and appreciated her for helping me through my tough times. She was a special lady!

With so many of my running mates scattered around the country, and with Larry Scarborough gone, I began to appreciate my classmates much more than I had in the past, and my admiration for them is stronger today than it has ever been. At this point in time, we have lost none of our classmates, and this seems to be pretty special, for all the classes above ours at Linville High and most of those classes several years younger have lost members due to health reasons, accidental death, or military death.

There would be an event that would be revealed in the middle of my senior year at Linville High, that came as a shock to many, including myself, and to others it was only a mild surprise, but there were only about four people that were aware of what was coming. Mrs. Hobgood managed the annual yearbook staff, The Stinger, it was called, as our school ball teams were known as 'The Hornets'. Shirley McKinnie was the yearbook Editor, Johnnie McKinnie was the Business Manager, and Bobby Jenny the Advertising Manager, and to my knowledge, Mrs. Hobgood, along with these three students were the four who knew the story of the final addition to the book for 1963.

The last page in the yearbook was a full page picture of Larry Scarborough's last class photo in The Stinger, and at the top of the picture "In Memoriam" was printed and at the bottom was "Larry Wayne Scarborough" and "January 10, 1944 – June 12, 1962". This was such a shock to many because Larry had dropped out of school after his junior year, mainly because of his heartbreak over Justin Cooper leaving Linville, plus the fact that Larry had been known to be a bit of a rebel. Many people assumed that the memorial to Larry Scarborough would not have been approved by the Linville High School Principal, Mr. Alton Hollis, because of Larry's reputation, and because he had been a high school dropout. Mr. Hollis was a straight laced leader, who was a Christian, a good man and a good teacher, someone who always strived to maintain a high standard for Linville High and all it stood for. The common thought was that even though Mr. Hollis was sympathetic to Larry Scarborough's family, and though he was saddened by his death, he still would not have approved of the memorial. But to insure that this did not happen, Mrs. Hobgood and those three leaders of the annual staff kept the memorial a secret from everyone else, and I personally do not know of anyone who was offended by the Memoriam picture.

The fact that this was orchestrated by Mrs. Hobgood, with the secrecy involved to make it happen, made me such a huge fan of this lady, one who rubbed quite a few people the wrong way. I was already so grateful to Mrs. Hobgood for helping to convince Mr. Hollis and others to arrange for me to be able to graduate, but after honoring my friend as she did, there was no way I would ever forget her, and I would love her for her compassion and showing her love for a troubled young man. She showed me that she understood that none of us were perfect, and that each of us deserved respect for the good in us, and that the troubled youths needed her compassion even more that those who were her favorite students for their drive and the ideals they shared.

I secretly shed a tear after receiving my copy of our yearbook and finding Larry's Memoriam in the book. I was so overwhelmed and overjoyed after seeing this, and it would be something that I would always hang onto, the same as the rest of my memories of Larry and the times we shared with the others who made up our little group of friends. Larry had many friends, and I know that all of his really close friends were so appreciative of the fact that he had been honored by Linville High. In the years since my final year at Linville High, I regard the Memoriam to Larry Scarborough as the main reason for my fondness of the 1963 Stinger, over and above all the notes written in it from my friends who were classmates and others from the grades below, and over any honors or pictures of basketball and baseball teams I was a member of. This final tribute to Larry from Linville High School meant so much to Larry's family and his many friends, but especially to those of us who were so close to him.

CHAPTER 18

A Journey, Then to Now

AFTER I DECIDED to write Larry Scarborough's story, I knew that without Justin Cooper's input, it would be impossible for me to accomplish this task. A year ago, we purchased new home office furniture and Diane, my wife, while sorting through our papers, throwing out that which we no longer needed, had found two sheets of legal sized copy paper, yellowed with age and folded in half, with some handwritten words, and she asked me what it was. When I opened the fold gingerly because of the age of the paper, I was surprised to find that it was my first effort of telling Larry Scarborough's story, as fiction because I had no idea of how to find Justin, and apparently, I had abandoned the project because that hurdle appeared to be too much for me to overcome at the time.

After completing the story about my father, and where that took me in the first nine years of my life with my first book, *Souvenirs of a Childhood Interrupted*, published in April of 2015, I decided that I had to locate Justin Cooper, and with her help in learning as much as I could about her relationship with Larry Scarborough, I would be able to do this story. But little did I know where it would lead me, and how long it would take me to find Justin and to gather enough information to complete my story. I basically knew the whole story except for the time when Justin and Larry fell in love, and their time spent together before Justin left Linville, Louisiana, when she returned to live with her grandmother in Baton Rouge. I spent so much time with Larry through his approximately sixteen months of heartbreak after Justin left, and I watched him suffer, marking it down in my memory, knowing that somehow, someday, I would tell the world the story of my friend, Larry Scarborough.

In July of 2015, I found on Facebook, a Ritchie Cox, and I knew from talking with Justin's sister, Grace Marie Harris, that Justin had a son named Richard Cox, and they had been living in the area north of Houston, Texas that included Montgomery County. This Ritchie Cox's profile on Facebook said he lived in New Caney, Texas, so I sent a Facebook message to Ritchie, not knowing whether it would reach him, as I was not friends with him on Facebook. I told him that Justin Cooper went to Linville High School in Linville, Louisiana for a short time in the early sixties, and I wanted to know if she was related to him. And sixteen months later, in November of 2016, I received a reply from Ritchie that said, "Yes, she's my mother."

Prior to receiving Ritchie's reply, my wife and I had made a couple of trips to Montgomery County, Texas, to addresses I had obtained through search engines on the internet, one trip to New Caney, Texas and one to Porter, Texas. Both trips had resulted in our finding that Justin and her son had lived at those locations several years before, and her daughter and granddaughter had lived with them in one place. After two trips from northeast Louisiana to southeast Texas with virtually no luck in gathering information that would help me locate Justin, I was to the point of giving up my search, and that meant that I would never be able to complete my story about Larry Scarborough.

When I received the message from Ritchie Cox, I asked to be friends on Facebook with him, and after he confirmed this, I sent a message to him explaining why I was looking for Justin, and I gave him my two telephone numbers and asked if he would give them to Justin. About a week later, I received a brief message from Ritchie that read, "O.K., I will give her the message," and that was it.

I told Diane that this Ritchie was a man of few words, and about a week after I received the message from him, I received a phone call from Justin, and we had a great visit, talking for about forty five minutes, and she was very receptive to my desire to do this story. I was on cloud nine, knowing that with her help, I would be able to fill the gap in the story I had been wanting to write for forty years, that gap being the few months during the courtship of Larry and Justin.

In early December of 2015, Diane and I had driven to Denham Springs, Louisiana, to meet Grace Marie Harris, Justin's sister, and while we were there, Justin's daughter, Kelley Wolfe, came by to see Grace Marie. We were thrilled to meet Kelley, who is a nurse, and she told us that she had not heard from her mother in over twenty two years.

Grace Marie told me a lot of the family history when we visited with her, in addition to our phone conversations since that time. After I located Justin, we talked numerous times, and I learned a lot about their childhood years. The Cooper girls' grandfather and grandmother were Sidney George and John Ella Kelley Cooper, who owned a one hundred acre farm in Hope Villa on Bayou Manchac, southeast of Baton Rouge, and Grace Marie and Justin's uncle and aunt owned eighty acres which adjoined the Cooper farm. They attended high school in Baton Rouge, but they lived on the farm in Hope Villa, where there were cows and horses, and Justin said they could ride the horses over the 180 acres, and she said it was great.

When I asked Justin about the spelling of her grandmother's first name, she told me that it was spelled J o h n, and her grandmother would get upset with anyone who spelled it differently. She said that Grandmother John Ella more or less raised her and Grace Marie after their mother remarried five years after the death of their Dad, Justin Claude Cooper.

There has been so much tragedy in the Cooper sister's lives that began before Justin was born. As I told you earlier, their maternal grandmother died from injuries she received from being kicked in the head by a horse two months before Justin Claude Cooper died in the car wreck.

On May 17, 2007, at the age of twenty six, Kelley's son, Cody, Justin's grandson, died in an automobile accident in the Baton Rouge area. Five months after Cody's death, Grace Marie's oldest son's child, Aaron Harris, died in an automobile accident just a few days after he had turned eighteen. Grace Marie's and Justin's half-sister, Carolyn, died of cancer ten months after Cody's death. Carolyn was their mother's daughter with her second husband, Murphy Langras, and she was only fifty five years old when she died.

Tragedy struck the family once again five years after Grace Marie's first grandson died, and this was when her youngest son's eighteen year old, Brice Harris, died on December 10, 2012, on his way to school when his pickup truck wheels dropped off the edge of the pavement. The truck hit a pipe protruding approximately six inches above the ground just beyond the shoulder of the road, which threw the truck into a tree. He was driving on a highway with a forty five mile per hour speed limit, and the point of impact with the tree was the driver's side door, and the young man died at the scene.

Grace Marie told me that a man driving just ahead of her grandson that morning, saw in his rear view mirror what had happened, and he stopped and ran back to the truck, and as he opened the door, the young man's bible fell out of the truck to the ground. He was wearing a tie and school colors for a school ball game trip from Denham Springs to Breaux Bridge, Louisiana on that day. I felt Grace Marie's sadness as she told me this story, and as she told me what a good and decent young man he was.

There was also much tragedy in the Scarborough family, beginning with Larry Scarborough's death, and many years later tragedy struck again, as Clint and Myrt Scarborough's son-in-law died in his burning pickup truck on a graveled road one night. Later, Larry's father took his own life in 1992 after suffering from a stroke a couple of years prior to this. Larry's younger brother, Doyle, then lost his wife to a heart attack on May 13, 2001, when she was only fifty four years old. On January 3, 2011, Doyle's son-in-law died in an automobile accident near Haile, Louisiana, and after an autopsy was performed, it was revealed that he actually died of a heart attack, which caused his vehicle to leave the road.

After my research revealed to me that which I did not already know about Larry and Justin, these two young people who loved each other fiercely for a brief period of time in the early sixties with a love that would never die, it is almost unbelievable to think that their families would have to suffer so much tragedy in their time on this earth.

CHAPTER 19

Closure Never Comes

AFTER TALKING WITH Justin a number of times by phone, Diane and I planned to visit with her in Alvarado, Texas, where she and Ritchie lived with Jamie Cox, who is Ritchie's older sister. Jamie has a ten year old daughter who is a special needs child, as she is almost totally deaf, but she is also a very sweet girl, according to a former landlady in Porter, Texas. In mid-January of 2017, when I called to set up a meeting with Justin, she told me that she and Ritchie had their belongings packed, and they were preparing to move back to New Caney, Texas. I put my plans on hold in order to give Justin and Ritchie ample time to find a residence after they moved back to Montgomery County, and time for them to get settled in.

Ritchie was having some problems and he had been in the hospital several times when they were in Alvarado, so Justin was busy in trying to get help for him both physically and financially, so I continued to visit with Justin by phone during the next few months. By doing so, I gathered the information I needed to continue writing this story, after putting it on hold for so long.

Justin and James (Jimmy) Cox were married June 7, 1976, and split up after twenty plus years of marriage. They only had the two children, Jamie, who was born April 8, 1977, and Richard, who was born November 1, 1978. They had a marriage that saw good times and bad times, but they just eventually grew apart and divorced. Jimmy's health was never very good, he had heart surgery when he was a child, and he continued to have some heart problems, along with other health issues. Justin told me he was always jealous, and she told me that if they were sitting at a bar and some guy came in and sat on the barstool next to her, Jimmy would get up and drag her stool, with her still sitting on it, over as close to his stool as he could get it.

Justin told me that her stepfather, Murphy Langras, had died November 28, 1989, at the age of sixty seven, and her mother, Marie, who died shortly afterwards, February 17, 1990, of an apparent heart attack. Murphy had been a good husband to Marie after their being divorced and then being reunited. When he died, maybe after losing two husbands she loved, Marie did not want to go on after Murphy passed away.

After Justin's divorce from Jimmy, she lived mostly in Montgomery County, Texas, struggling to get by over the years due to helping her children even after they were grown, which contributed to her struggles. There was a long period of time where Justin seemed to just turn her back on the life she had in the Baton Rouge area, and this included leaving her first born, Kelley, in her past, along with her sister, Grace Marie. Justin's family was unable to locate her when her grandson, Cody, died in 2007, and after her half-sister, Carolyn, passed away ten months after Cody's death, Justin's step-brother, Danny Langras, searched for three months before finally making contact with Justin. After Danny gave Justin the news of her grandson's death and her sister's death, he was unable to get in touch with Justin again until Christmas of 2016, when he called her at the number I had obtained.

Grace Marie told me that Justin was always a good girl, and that she was just wild, but she had been baptized at the age of ten, so she knew she was alright, wherever she was. She said that Justin seemed to have some family struggles that she had to endure, as many of us have, and Grace assumed that this was the reason they had lost touch with one another. Grace Marie told me of the good times they had as girls, and how much their grandmother had meant to them. Their grandmother, John Ella Cooper, made sure the girls were always in church with her on Sunday and again on Wednesday night when they lived with her. After John Ella died when Grace Marie was twenty years old and Justin was nineteen, the sisters drifted away from church since their Mother figure was gone. Today, Grace Marie is an active Christian lady who continues to attend church regularly, and Justin seemed to drift away from church, but she continues to have faith.

My contact with Justin confirmed my belief that circumstances beyond her control in 1961 led to mistakes that she made, such as the pregnancy and the hasty marriage to Charles Hinton. And after living with Charles only seven months, she gave birth to Kelley as a single mother, and in just a few short months after that, the one chance that she had for true happiness in her life, re-joining Larry Scarborough, did not happen because of one phone call. The call Larry made on the night he died resulted in disaster, because he wound up talking to a stranger who did not know him or anything about him. The fact that Larry would not tell Grace Marie's friend who he was, and his failure to tell the young lady his connection with Justin and his love for her, contributed to that failure in communications. And Larry Scarborough's death, the result of that failure, brought with it the end to any chance of the reuniting of the two young lovers.

I personally believe that had things gone as they should have on that fateful night, there would not have been a heartbroken Larry Scarborough driving up Highway 71 after midnight, but a happy young man who would have been looking forward to the next day, when he would have called Grace Marie's apartment, where Justin sat waiting for his call. Justin told me that she expected that call after getting the message that Larry was in town when she came home to Grace Marie's that night. The next morning, she skipped the business school she was attending at the time, excitedly waiting for Larry to call.

But the call Justin received came not that morning from Larry, but from Parker Haile, from Haile, Louisiana that afternoon, informing her that Larry had died in a car crash near Bunkie, Louisiana, shortly after midnight. Justin was devastated upon hearing that Larry was gone, the only man she had ever truly loved, gone, and with him her chance for happiness, and left in its place, a longing that would never leave her, as she would go through the motions of trying to live with this tragic turn of events.

As Justin and I talked during the final phone conversation before I completed Larry's story, when I told her of Armond Love's comments about seeing her and Larry at the Hooker Hole on the Ouachita River, and he could tell how much they loved one another by the expressions on their faces when they touched one another. Justin told me that this was true.... it was just MAGIC!

When I told Justin during this same conversation about Larry's love for Ray Charles' two songs, *Born to Lose,* and *I Can't Stop Loving You,* in the few months prior to his death, it brought so much of that period of time back to me, the times when we were together with our friends. *Born to Lose* haunted me for a time because it seemed so prophetic in Larry's case, but the other song hit me as the real truth when I heard it so many times in the ensuing years. Many years after hearing these songs for the first time, I purchased a boxed set of CD's of Ray Charles songs, and one CD had those songs on it. This significance of *I Can't Stop Loving You* had been apparent to me since shortly after it was released in the spring of 1962, for it stated the words that Larry felt about Justin Cooper, "I Can't Stop Loving You".

As for me, Larry, my friend, I speak for myself, but I know in my heart there are other friends who feel the same way about you, and that is the fact that we can't stop loving you as our friend. I also told Justin this in that final conversation before I completed Larry's story.

Justin answered all my questions I held for so many years that were stored away until the time when I located her and talked with her. When I asked her if she understood how I felt, she replied, "I certainly do!"

She told me that she had pondered over time all the variations of the question "what if?" when she thought of Larry Scarborough. "I really loved Larry and I know my life would have been so, so different if we had reconnected. And we would have reconnected if only Larry had talked with Grace that night he called for me, because she had met Larry on one occasion, and she would have given him the information that would have prevented him from leaving Baton Rouge that night."

Justin then summed it all up in her final statement to me, "If were able to speak to Larry today, after all this time, and after hearing the rest of his story from you, what I would say to him is, "Larry, my love, *I Can't Stop Loving You!*"

Justin Cooper
"Lady"

In Memoriam

LARRY WAYNE SCARBOROUGH
January 10, 1944 – June 12, 1962

ACKNOWLEDGEMENTS

First of all, I would like to thank Justin Cooper Cox for telling me her story of the key portion of this book, and that is the time she met and fell in love with Larry Scarborough. Without her help, I could not have completed this story that I waited so long to write.

Two others who contributed greatly are Shirley Traylor, who edited my story, and Bobby Jenny, who has shared with me the love of observing people in our past and appreciating their contributions to our memories.

Others who gave me valuable input are Betty Scarborough Baker, Doyle Scarborough, Billy Tom Ellis, Billy George McKinnie, Sidney Ray, Bobbie Lee Roberson, Paul Meeks, Tommy Joe Jenny, Armond Love and Jerry Owens. I would also like to thank Grace Marie Harris, who gave me so much of the Cooper family history.

Most of all, I would like to thank those who read my first book, *Souvenirs of a Childhood Interrupted*, and encouraged me to write another. Their belief in my ability was the impetus for me to persevere until I gathered the information I needed to fill the gaps in this story that I needed to write, after all this time.

CPSIA information can be obtained
at www.ICGtesting.com
Printed in the USA
FFOW02n0053240518
46858841-49083FF